To Fu Doo.

Success is not the key to Happiness.
Happiness is the key to Success.

Best Regards
Jork

UNDERSTANDING QUANTUM THINKING

MARK DAWES

The Derwent Press
Derbyshire, England
www.derwentpress.com

UNDERSTANDING QUANTUM THIKING
BY
MARK DAWES

All Rights Reserved.
© NFPS Ltd 2008

All rights reserved. No part of this book may be reproduced, stored in a retrieval system, or transmitted, in any form or by any means, electronic, mechanical, photocopying, recording and/or otherwise without the prior permission of Mark Dawes. All company logos and trademarks etc. are the property of Mark Dawes and are not to be used or adapted by any individual or organisation. This book may not be lent, resold, hired out or otherwise disposed of by way of trade in any form, binding or cover other than that in which it is published, without prior consent of Mark Dawes.

ISBN 10: 1-84667-035-7
ISBN 13: 978-1-84667-035-0

BOOK DESIGN BY:
PAM MARIN-KINGSLEY, WWW.FAR-ANGEL.COM

Published in 2008
by
The Derwent Press
Derbyshire, England
www.derwentpress.com

CONTENTS

Preface: The Great Paradox by Barry WinBolt 9

Chapter 1: My Story 13

Chapter 2: How We Make Sense of Our World 23

Chapter 3: Body Language—Your Body Believes Every Word You Say 33

Chapter 4: The Groove Theory of Habitual Behaviour 44

Chapter 5: How Thoughts Become Things 61

Chapter 6: The Law of Attraction and Interaction 71

Chapter 7: Fall Seven times—Stand Up Eight 84

Chapter 8: Beliefs 92

Chapter 9: Stress 102

Chapter 10: Learned Helplessness 116

Chapter 11: Happiness Now 124

Chapter 12: Money Grows on Trees 135

Endnote 143

About the Author 147

PREFACE:
THE GREAT PARADOX

Some of us feel, on a good day, that we have a reasonable degree of control over our lives; that we have a fair chance of reaching our goals, enjoying success, security and happiness. Others say that we have very little control; that we are at the whim of events, fate, chance, or worse, somebody else.

Realistically of course none of us can claim to have total control over every aspect of our lives, but having a sense of personal agency or personal mastery is said to have a positive effect on our psychological well-being and our health. So anything that helps us improve on our sense of personal mastery and give us a realistic guidance on how to move towards greater fulfillment and success is welcome.

I think that *Understanding Quantum Thinking* does just that. As I read it I became increasingly aware of an image that was forming for me—like the parts of a jigsaw puzzle clicking into place—of a map that would provide directions for my day-to-day thinking and planning. Mind you, there are plenty of books that do that, Mark Dawes goes further, he provides the nudges and prompts to help us change our thinking habits, so being more productive becomes an automatic and unconscious process.

Most of us would like to be thought of as individuals, and the freedom to choose the sort of lives we live. The great paradox of contemporary life is that the more we strive for individuality, the less we able we are to develop as individuals. In parallel with this, the more choice we have, the less we are free to choose. I think *Understanding Quantum Thinking* provides a basis for understanding these conundrums. It provides us with a framework that can actually allow us to express our individuality and give us greater choice in how we live our lives.

Individuality and choice, we are told, are cornerstones of freedom, and freedom—if you listen to the political and social rhetoric—is good. As we look around though, we cannot fail to notice that we are constantly limited in what we do, because governments and systems require us to comply and so limit our freedom. People who really express their individuality are seen as odd, or a threat to the system. So conformity is rewarded, and our thinking politely complies.

Where choice is concerned, we hear so often that choice is good, and so more choice must be better. This has become one of the mantras of modern times. Yet, the greater the range of goods and services we are offered, the more they are standardized in the name of efficiency and profit. Real choice is limited to what is provided for us. As a simple example, think of how the major supermarkets—who provide so much of our consumables—mimic and copy each other as they vie for our attention and our loyalty.

Lifestyle choices are similarly limited by practicalities, to what is available and what is considered acceptable. What we often fail to notice is the way in which our thinking is constrained by the same influences, so that few of us can really say that we think freely about what we want and how we want to be. We may dream, but simply by framing hopes and ambitions as dreams, we risk placing them out of our reach, because few dreams become reality.

In *Understanding Quantum Thinking*, Mark describes how we are slaves to our habits and prisoners of our beliefs. He also shows how we can move forward in our lives, each in our own, unique way, by training our thinking and transforming our thoughts into tangible results.

We are a social species so it is natural that we should conform, but within our societies we equally want to grow and develop as individuals. This book is a gem because, succinctly and with a minimum of fuss, Mark shows us first what the problem is then suggests what to do about it. We can reclaim our lives, express our individuality and exercise choice, but first we need to examine our beliefs and shake up how we think.

The result, if we follow his advice, will be another paradox. These pages show that we have the potential to remodel our lives, inspiring ourselves and those around us to do better. The paradox is that in flowering as individuals we will make fairer and more cohesive communities, to the benefit of society as a whole.

Mark has a unique way of drawing complex ideas together into a simple, accessible and powerful message. This makes his book not only a delight to read, but a compendium of practical advice on living better, and making the change we seek effective. Part of its value is, I believe, that it is deceptive in its apparent simplicity. It can be read quickly, even superficially, yet as a work of philosophy it is a text to jolt us out of complacency in our thinking.

This book is an inspiration, but don't just take my word for it, read it, and notice your reactions to it.

Barry Winbolt
November 2008

CHAPTER 1.
MY STORY

I was brought up in a typical middle-class family in West London. I was one of six children, and although we never had a lot of money, we were happy.

I enjoyed school, but not really for the education, I enjoyed the social life and the friends I had and, as a result, I ended up leaving school with two O'Levels and one CSE Grade 1. I possibly could have done better, but from an early age, I was intent on joining the Royal Marines so I didn't see the need to study for 'academic stuff'. I was going to be a warrior, a trained killer with a green beret! Unfortunately, my mother had other ideas and was against me being a Royal Marine. In her mind, she saw me being killed, so I ended up joining the Royal Navy—drowning is possibly a preferred way of death in my family!

I thoroughly enjoyed being in the Navy, however, I enjoyed having fun too much and didn't take myself, or what I considered to be punitive discipline too seriously, as the following extract from one of my leadership reports shows:

> *Dawes enjoys the variety and comradeship of Service life... He was a regular, if rather shallow contributor to classroom debate: his inputs were rapidly expressed with a number of throw-away phrases, revealing a cheerfully uncomplicated outlook. A programmed re-arrangement foreshortened the preparation of his lecturette, but given that the change was forced upon him, his poor showing demonstrated a reliance on last minute preparation. The talk was hurriedly delivered, poorly illustrated and fell short of the time allocated... On the parade ground his personal drill and bearing need to be smarter... Very fit on arrival, he worked cheerfully and well during the physical programme to make an improvement in his standard*

> *... Dawes is a friendly, cheerfully open young man, who at first was rather too jaunty and superficial."*

However, in spite of others wanting me to consider my career more seriously, I wasn't prepared to compromise my lifestyle—having fun, if you like—for the sake of a 'serious career'. I loved the life—signing on for nine years service when I reached eighteen and as soon as I was eligible I extended that by signing on for a full twenty-two year career.

In spite of my *jaunty* outlook I eventually ended up getting commissioned from the ranks to become a Naval Officer in 1985. However, I ended my service after twelve years as a Naval Officer, following a disagreement with Senior Officers.

During my time in the Royal Navy I had become accustomed to having everything found and done for me in terms of accommodation, food, clothing and bills. All I had to do was my job and collect my pay cheque at the end of each month. Even my tax was paid for me. However, like most of us in the service I always had more month left at the end of the money, and why shouldn't I? I was planning to stay in for a full career and at the end of that I would leave with a full pension. Life was planned out and sorted, at least up until the point that I decided to leave.

When I actually left the Navy I was four thousand pounds in debt (a lot of money in 1988). I also had no idea how to survive in the outside world—the land of the 'civvi'. As a result of my financial limitations I ended up living in a rented room that was so small I actually had to cut the end off my bed to get it to fit in the room, and I had to sleep with my legs bent every night. This was a bit of a culture shock. With no money to fall back on I also had to find work just to make ends meet. This was far removed from the Naval Officers accommodation that I had left behind.

However, within two years of leaving the service I was working as a computer salesman, and out of a sales staff of over twelve I was personally generating over a third of the company's sales myself, becoming, in a relatively short period of time, the second highest paid computer salesperson in the UK for that particular computer group. What was really interesting was that I couldn't even work the computers I was selling! As a result of my new found wealth my wife and I bought a large house in West London with a big garden and things were going really well.

Then I made my first big error. I decided to buy a little business and it nearly cost me everything. I ended up losing all of the money I had earned and was earning. It even looked as if my home was about to be re-possessed. I even had to sell my car one month to pay the wage bill. How could this happen? The truth was it was my fault. I didn't keep my eye on the business. Had it not been for my wife's job and her income, and the help of a financial expert (my good friend Nigel) we would have probably lost the house.

After that I needed to find a job that would give me a regular salary, so I became a prison officer. Now, just as before, I was enjoying the fun and comradeship of uniformed life, however, financially I was earning less than twenty percent of what I had previously earned, so that was a wake–up call, but it was enough for us to get by on and that, together with my wife's income, helped us clear the debt that had built up a result of my previous failed business venture.

Then one of those defining moments happened when you realise that life, as you have come to know it, was about to change. Colin, one of the guys I was training with at the prison service college, gave me a set of audiotapes to listen to. He had bought them and thought they were a bit *'American'*, a bit *'happy-clappy'*, and to use his words, a bit *'wanky'*, so he passed them on to me. At first I had to agree with Colin. They were a bit *'American'* and a bit *'happy-clappy'*, but if you got through that, then the actual information was pretty interesting. What interested me most of all was not only that this guy on these tapes was making sense, but also what he was saying just seemed too simple to be true. The obvious test to find out whether or not what he was saying worked was to do what he was advising.

So, secretly I started listening to the tapes more intently, following the advice, writing out my goals, dreams and affirmations, using my imagination to construct images in my mind of what I wanted to acquire, focusing only on what I wanted and not on what I didn't want, and the strangest thing was that things started to change. I became the top student of my entry in the prison service college that year. Within another year I was selected to become a Hostage Negotiator and I also opened a local martial arts school teaching ju-jitsu. This led to me being approached by a local Police Officer, a lovely man (who has since become a good friend) called John Gridley, who asked me to get involved with local crime prevention issues. As a result of that I attended local meetings and that led to me being asked by a couple of very large national companies to run training courses for their staff. All of this I did part time using my weekends and days off from the prison service to run courses. One of these companies ended up being a client of mine for over five years.

My motivation was that I never wanted to be put in a situation again where I would be financially broke. Not poor, that is a mindset and not a situation or set of circumstances, but broke (and there is a difference).

Eventually I was earning more money part-time then I was earning full time from my prison service career and it became time once again to make a choice. Carry on the way I was, relying on the security of my prison service career and the regular income it generated (albeit a relatively low income) and the eventual pension it would provide, or go it alone. All the well-meaning advice I was getting from my colleagues in the service, with the exception of a few close friends, was to stay in my regular 'wage-prison' service job. *"The job is for life,"* some would say, *"Think of your pension,"* others would say, *"What if you fail and get in debt again?"* was another solemn bit of advice that made the decision all the more harder. But the reality was that I couldn't see myself being a prison officer for the rest of my working life. What it offered was too limiting for me.

Those initial tapes that had been given to me by a well-meaning friend, the subsequent books I had read as a result of those tapes and the additional audio material I bought and listened to, had made me want more from life. In short I wanted to live my life, not just trudge through the process of making a living. As Anthony Robbins said on those first tapes I was given, *'Design a life, don't just make a living.'*

So the decision was made, and with the support of my wife, I left my job in the prison service and started my own business. I was convinced and disciplined in my thinking that if I focussed only on what I wanted and didn't waste time focussing on what I didn't want, I would draw information, events and circumstances to me to make my goals and dreams happen. I decided to invest in myself by broadening and deepening my knowledge at every opportunity. Having never really been someone who liked reading books, almost overnight, I became an avid reader. I bought and listened to hundreds of audio-books and I attended many seminars and training events, some better than others, but I believed that if each thing I did could give me one bit of information that I could use then it was a good investment and not a waste of time.

Then one day I attended a seminar event on *'Managing Angry People'* which I found fascinating. However, the day itself didn't go as far as I would have liked it to go in terms of the subject matter I was specifically looking for. So at the end of the seminar I took the time to stay behind and talk to the speaker. The result of that conversation led to me being invited to become a speaker for the organisation concerned and I ended up doing eighteen seminars around the UK to audiences of between 30–300 people. This was a great opportunity, which not only provided me with a very nice income, but one that raised my professional profile in the industry. The experience also taught me a lot about how people learn.

What I learned was that people do not only want information or knowledge, they also want to be entertained. So if you can provide knowledge with a bit of fun, then people will not only remember you, but they will also retain a lot more information as opposed to just sitting there and passively taking it in. So I learned that if I could help people create a positive state they will learn in a much more efficient and enjoyable way.

Now this isn't rocket science. Many of you will remember the Open University programmes that used to be shown on BBC2 at about 5am in the morning, delivered primarily by strange looking bearded men in equally strange jumpers. Now these were very highly intelligent people but in short, they were also highly boring.

So the initial business model was born. Give people something that will not only help them but that they will enjoy as well. If we can do this then the atmosphere we are going to be working in will be more enjoyable for us too. So basically, in taking a leaf out of Tony Robbins vocabulary, we made our vacation our vocation and to this day my business partner and I don't go to work—we go on holiday!

Then one day I was reading a book written by Sue Knight entitled *NLP in Business*, and I thought let's do another NLP course. I already had experience of Neuro-Linguistic Programming, but I hadn't really applied it, so I thought it was about time that I went and did some more training so I enrolled on a course. On the first day I hated it so much that I nearly came home, but something made me stay and I'm glad I did because it turned out to be fascinating stuff. I then furthered my training in this field and as a result I met someone who was a qualified hypnotherapist, which made me consider becoming a hypnotherapist myself. It wasn't something I had consciously thought of doing but it intrigued me, so I thought I'd follow my 'gut-feeling' and enrol on a course.

Eventually I qualified as a cognitive hypnotherapist. I had never intended to become a therapist, as I don't do therapy *per se*. My prime agenda for attending all of these courses was two-fold: One, to help me develop my skills to become a better trainer, speaker and physical skills coach, and secondly, to continually help me find ways of improving the quality of life for my family and myself.

Not long after that a guy called Trevor Silvester who runs the Quest Institute[1], which I think is one of the best hypnotherapy and NLP training organisations in the UK, suggested that I watch a DVD called *What the Bleep do we Know?* which is a film about quantum mechanics. I found the movie absolutely mind blowing. What it basically did was provide scientific evidence and proof that underpinned everything that I had been doing and studying over the previous few years, and having always been a bit of a 'doubting Thomas' this was exactly what I needed. More importantly, it came along at exactly the right time. It spurred me on a search to find out more about the field of quantum mechanics and how this universal science affects each and every one of us at every level.

The more I learned about quantum mechanics, the more things started to make sense to me in relation to some of the so-called coincidences that I had been experiencing in my life. For example, at one time a particular book was consistently being brought to my attention. I'd walk into a bookshop and out of the thousands of books on the shelves I'd notice this particular book. Then I'd be at an airport waiting to fly somewhere and once again I'd notice the

---

1. The Quest Institute: www.questinstitute.co.uk

very same book. This wasn't just a coincidence; this was a signal for me that this book had something that was relevant or important to me. In the past I would have looked at it, possibly picked it up, looked at the price and more than likely, put it back. Now I tend to trust my instinct more and act on it.

On another occasion I was recently asked to speak at a national conference on violence at work and noticing that the previous speaker had put the audience to sleep, I decided to wake them up by giving them a few mind-blowing facts about what I had learned about quantum mechanics as part of my introduction. Interestingly, I was there to promote my mainstream business but as a result of that one or two minute introduction I was asked if I did NLP. This led to me being engaged by the organisation to run a range of courses on the subject of positive thinking, NLP and quantum mechanics. This led to another organisation hearing about what I was doing who then subsequently commissioned me to run a large number of courses for them too. Had I not acted on my instincts and attended that initial NLP course this opportunity may never have arisen. I am now running similar courses all over the UK for other organisations both large and small and enjoying every minute of it.

Now here's the interesting, or spooky part, depending on your own personal perspective. As I began to look back along the timeline of my life, from where I've come from and from the experiences I have had along the way, I've begun to realise that there are no such things as coincidences. Everything I am is a product of my experience in life. If I hadn't had these experiences, I wouldn't be writing this book now.

Deepak Chopra is a very well-respected medical doctor and writer who sums up the issue of coincidences in his book, entitled *Synchrodestiny*,[2] by inviting the reader to take part in an experiment. What he writes is this:

> *Close your eyes and think about what you've been doing over the past twenty-four hours. Then move backward through your memory from where you are right now to where you were exactly one day ago. In your mind's eye,*

---

2. *Synchrodestiny* by Deepak Chopra, Rider & Co (07/2005), ISBN 184413219-6.

conjure up as much detail as you can about the things you did, the thoughts that passed through your mind, and the feelings that affected your heart.

As you do this pick one theme or subject from the past twenty-four hours and focus on that particular thought. It doesn't have to be anything especially important or spectacular—just something that you remember dealing with during the day. If you went to the bank, you might choose money or finances. If you had a doctor's appointment, you could choose health. If you played golf or tennis, you could focus on athletics. Consider this theme for a few seconds.

Now, think back five years. Concentrate on today's date, and then work back, year by year, until you reach the same date five years ago. See if you can recall more or less where you were and what you were doing at the time. Try to picture your life at that moment as clearly as you can.

Once you have created a clear mental image of your life as it was five years ago, introduce the theme or subject that you chose to focus on from the past twenty-four hours—finances, health, religion, whatever it was. Now, track your involvement with that subject over the past five years and right up to the present. Try to remember as many incidents as you can in that particular area of your life. If you've chosen health as your topic, for example, you might remember any illness you've had, how they might have led you from one doctor to another, how you may have decided to stop smoking and how that may have affected various areas of your life, or the diet you chose, or any of a thousand other possibilities. Go ahead and do this exercise now.

As you were thinking about your chosen subject, how it evolved in your life and how it affects the way you live now, I'm certain you discovered many "co-incidences."

So much of life depends on chance meetings, twists of fate, or pathways that suddenly branch out in a new direction. And it is likely that your one topic very quickly connected with many other areas of your life, even if the subject seemed totally insignificant at first. By tracing your personal history in this way you can gain enormous insight into the role that coincidence has played in your life. You can see how, if even one tiny detail had turned out differently, you might have ended up somewhere else, with different people, engaged in different work, moving on an entirely different life trajectory.

Even when you think you have your life all mapped out, things happen that shape your destiny in ways you might never have imagined. The coincidences or little miracles that happen every day of your life are hints that the universe has much bigger plans for you than you ever dreamed of for yourself.

The last paragraph of what Deepak Chopra wrote above was also 'coincidentally' summed up beautifully by Nelson Mandela, when he quoted Marianne Williamson in his inaugural speech in 1994:

Our deepest fear is not that we are inadequate. Our deepest fear is that we are powerful beyond measure. It is our light, not our darkness, that most frightens us. We ask ourselves, who am I to be brilliant, successful, talented and fabulous? Actually, who are you NOT to be? You are a child of God. Your playing small doesn't serve the world. There's nothing enlightened about shrinking so that other people won't feel insecure around you. We were born to make manifest the glory that is within us. It's not just in some of us; it's in EVERYONE! And as we let our own light shine, we unconsciously give other people permission to do the same. As we are liberated from our own fear, our presence automatically liberates others!

As a result of all of this, I can afford to do pretty much what I like in monetary terms. Now I'm not telling you this to impress you but more to impress upon you that if I can do it, anyone can. It's all about belief, passion, commitment and unwavering faith in focusing on what you want and trusting your instincts to bring you those things that you need to make it happen. If you consider that you only need a small amount of information out of all of the information available to us to design your destiny, you will soon be able to find it easier to notice much more easily those opportunities that will come your way that you possibly didn't notice before, simply because you weren't looking for them or because you were focusing your intentions or thoughts in the wrong direction.

This book therefore, is dedicated to you in the hope that you will begin to realise that you are the master of your destiny. All that occurs is down to what we do. All that we do is down to what we think about and what we think about brings about that which we experience. Therefore, if you want to change your life, to have more control over what you do and who you'll become, would like more control over your finances, your health and every aspect of your life, you have to start with the way you think.

In this book I have covered a number of different subjects that I lecture on and talk about regularly. I find them fascinating, as I hope you do too. Wherever I can, I have either listed or mentioned the book or other resource that I am referring to, should you wish to read it or refer to it yourself.

Finally trust your instincts. If you are being drawn towards a certain book pick it up, if you keep thinking about doing something, do it because there is possibly a reason for doing so. And if you consider that, there is also a reason you are reading this book now, and who knows where this may take you to next?

As Mahatma Ghandi once said:

> *Men often become what they believe themselves to be. If I believe I cannot do something, it makes me incapable of doing it. But when I believe I can, then I acquire the ability to do it even if I didn't have it in the beginning.*

CHAPTER 2.
HOW WE MAKE SENSE
OF OUR WORLD

There are only two primary ways we make sense of our world—consciously and unconsciously.

Our conscious mind is the part of our mind which we use actively and deliberately. For example, as you are reading this text you are focussing your conscious awareness towards taking in this information.

Our unconscious mind works in the background. It can process billions of bits of information every single second. It provides access to all of our wisdom, knowledge and memories and is the primary source of all of our creativity. It also runs all of our automatic behaviours that we do not need to pay conscious attention to. For example, while reading this your unconscious mind will be controlling your breathing rate and blood flow around you body. This is useful because if your breathing and blood flow had to be consciously monitored, you would possibly die every time you fell asleep. Our unconscious mind is also where all of our habitual behaviours are stored, behaviours that we once learned consciously. By having this unconscious ability we can free our conscious minds up to think about other things.

For example, when you first learned to drive a car or ride a bike, you were consciously aware of everything that you had to do, which actually made doing it all difficult! Now that you can drive a car or ride a bike you take much of the behaviour for granted as it is now habitual—you don't have to use a lot of conscious attention to do it.

According to the science of quantum mechanics, an area of science that has never been proved wrong in over eight decades, the brain processes approximately 400 billion bits of information per second that are coming in through all of our sense organs.

However, our minds filter only 2000 bits of information into our conscious awareness, and those 2000 bits that we are aware of are the most self-serving. In short, the small percentage of information that comes into our conscious awareness is the information we need to support what we believe or what we are focussing on or thinking about at any given moment in time.

What this actually means is that we are only actually aware of 0.0000000005% or only of 5/1000 of a million percent of all of the available information that is presented to us at any given moment in time. In other words there is an untapped void, a potentially infinite amount of information readily available to all of us outside of our normal realm of conscious attention which the vast majority of us do not access, or, more correctly put—do not know how to access.

In short many of us are living in a world where all we see is the tip of an immense quantum mechanical iceberg, where the realm of potential possibility and the void of infinite intelligence lies just beneath the surface.

If the brain is actually processing four-hundred billion bits of information per second, and our awareness is only on two thousand bits of information that means that reality is happening in the brain all of the time. In short the brain is receiving much more information than it can integrate.

That means that the vast majority of people walking around our world are simply doing nothing more than re-creating the same reality that they created yesterday, so tomorrow just becomes another day like today for them and they become blind to the potentially unlimited source of infinite intelligence that is available to all of us.

PERCEPTION V REALITY

Our eyes and our mind use the same parts of the visual cortex to process information. This means that when we close our eyes and visualise, the same parts of the visual cortex become active in the same way as they would if we we're seeing something directly in front of us. This means that our brains can't tell the difference between what we're experiencing in the external world and what we're imagining in our mind's eye. So if you ever wake up sweating and breathing heavily from a nightmare, it is because the brain has perceived the situation as being real and therefore, has triggered the body's fight-or-flight response into action (more on that later).

In the film entitled *What the Bleep do we know*, that I mentioned in the previous chapter, the issue of perception and reality is discussed and what the film communicates, based on proven science, is very interesting. They state that the brain doesn't know the difference between what we see with the eyes and what we see with the brain. As a result many of us have been conditioned to believe that the external world, that which we see through our eyes, is more real than the internal world, that which we create in our minds. The science of quantum mechanics however, has proved that what is happening within us will create what's happening outside of us. In short, the reality of what we experience on a day-to-day basis is a direct result of what we expect to experience based on our cumulative perceptions of previous experience.

The film goes on to state that scientific experiments have shown that if they take a person and connect them up to sensitive and highly accurate biofeedback machines such as 'PET' or 'MRI' scanners, and then ask the person to look at a certain object, scientists can watch certain areas of the person's brain light up. They then ask the subject to close their eyes and to imagine that same object, and when the subject imagines that same object, it produced the same areas of the brain to light up, as if they were actually visually looking at it. So this causes scientists to back up and ask the question, what do we see with? Does the brain see or do the eyes see? And what is reality, is reality what were seeing with our brain, or is reality what we seeing with our eyes? And the basic fundamental truth that is proved by the science is that the brain does not know the difference between what it sees in its environment and what it remembers because the same specific neurological networks are firing. This again raises the question: what is reality?

WE DON'T SEE WITH OUR EYES, WE SEE WITH OUR BRAINS[3]

Here is an interesting fact. There are approximately 7 million light cells in the eye, but there are around 100 million nerve cells in the first visual area in the brain that the nerve impulses from the eye reach. Why are there 100 cells available to process information from every single cell that receives light from the environment? Why would there be this massive overcompensation? The answer is that there isn't. The processing areas are doing something other than merely making something out of the light sent their way by the eye.

What actually happens is that light comes in through the eye and hits the retina. It's converted to electrical signals and shuttled to the brain where it is processed simultaneously by different parts of the visual cortex, parts responsible for movement, colour, etc. The image is then re-assembled, predominantly in the part of the brain called the thalamus, which is when we become consciously aware of seeing.

The thalamus has been described as the junction box of the brain because information received from the senses is sent to it, and from there it is disseminated to the other areas of the brain responsible for processing it. However, when these processed neural messages return to the thalamus they contain eighty percent more information than when they were initially sent out. Think about that, because this means that eighty percent of the world that we become consciously aware of comes from within our own mind. In essence, what this means is that we are responsible for making up most of the reality we experience in the world. We create it every day.

Think about that when you have the time because it's a big thought. It leads us to conclude that we project onto what is around us what we expect it to be. In a very real sense we're responsible for how things look. Try it out. If you go out on a clear evening and look up at the stars you're seeing light from billions of light years away. In short, you're seeing to the edge of the viewable universe.

---

3. Parts reprinted with kind permission of the Quest Institute, the home of Cognitive Hypnotherapy: www.questinstitute.co.uk.

But the view that is being projected is from within your brain. Your brain is creating the show.

In the words of Richard Gregory: *"Our sight consists of a hypothesis, an interpretation of the world. We do not see the data in front of our eyes; we see an interpretation."*

In other words, the brain is using past experience stored as memory, and anticipatory memory (an imagined future), as the basis for giving meaning to the information that flows into us from our environment. So we don't see what we sense, we see what we think we sense. This is because what we are experiencing moment by moment, has already been previously processed, or given meaning, by our brain. In short, by the time you perceive an object in front of you the brain has already decided its meaning.

THE QUANTUM VIEW

Quantum mechanics have given science a deep insight into the microscopic world that we exist in, and one of the most perplexing facts of quantum theory is that the reality of what we experience in our physical world depends entirely on our observation of it, and this principle, for many people, seems impossible to believe.

Quantum mechanics states that objects are created by observation of them. As a result the observer creates the reality of what exists. In other words, atoms and sub-atomic particles do not exist anywhere until they are observed. In short, everything exists in fields of unending possibilities and it is not until we observe that potential that the reality collapses into existence. As a result there is a scientific connection between conscious observation and the material world. Today all physicists generally accept the principle that quantum theory applies universally, and if that is so, then all reality is created by observation.

Now this is very, very big and phenomenally important. If reality does not exist independent of conscious observation then it has to be taken that observation creates everything, including ourselves, who we become and the lives we will ultimately live.

Now although quantum mechanics is relatively new, the principle is not necessarily a new phenomenon. The idea of physical reality being created by its observation goes back thousands of years to ancient Vedic philosophy.

THE MIND CANNOT PROCESS A NEGATIVE COMMAND

Our minds are also like filters, which do not compute negatives. As such it doesn't understand a negative command and cannot carry it out. What it does is simply interpret any input from a positive perspective.

For example, if I say, *"Don't think of blue trees,"* you have to actually think of them and then try and stop yourself doing it. In short the brain interprets the command as, *"Think of blue trees—don't."* For those of you with small children, you will have experienced this phenomenon before. When a child walks in a room balancing a glass of drink full to the brim, a parent may say, *"Don't drop that,"* but what the child's brain interprets is: *"Drop that—don't."* As a result the drink is spilt and a parent could end up reprimanding the child for the behaviour that was the direct result of the thought placed in the child's mind that was not there before.

Recently my daughter Katie was studying for her 'A' Levels. As a result the kitchen table was taken over as her workspace and was covered in her study books, journals, and her laptop. One day while she was working, my wife made mugs of tea for us and as I passed Katie's mug of tea to her I heard myself say: *"Mind you don't drop that over all your work."* Katie replied, in a slightly frustrated voice: *"Dad I've been sitting at this table working and drinking tea here now for nearly a year and I haven't spilt anything yet so I'm not likely to!"* Well, it was only a few minutes later when Katie bellowed from the kitchen: *Dad—you idiot—look what you made me do?"* Yes, you guessed it—she had managed to spill tea all over her work, something she had never done before and something that had possibly never even entered her mind until I planted the thought there. Even monkeys fall out of trees occasionally.

Another example was when I was asked to oversee some training. The instructor was teaching a physical skill to a group of new recruits. He gave a good introduction to what he wanted the group to do with regard to the skill demonstrating where they should correctly place their feet and hands. It was also clear that the group were eager to get on with practicing the skill. However, just before he let them go to practice he said this:

> "A common mistake that most people make when doing this technique is that they nearly always place their foot here instead of there. Now I don't want you to put your foot there. Make sure that it goes here. If I catch any of you putting your foot there I'll come down on you. There is absolutely no reason why it should be there. I'll be watching you and I bet that one of you will do exactly what I have just told you not to do. Right off you go."

Now as you can imagine most of the trainees will be more concerned with not wanting to get it wrong as opposed to getting it right for the possible fear of being singled out and embarrassed by the instructor. As a result most of the trainees will be more concerned, worried and therefore focussed, on what they mustn't do as opposed to what they should do. Within minutes, the instructor caught someone putting their foot exactly where they shouldn't. He called the group to stop what they were doing and then went on to further explain why they shouldn't put their foot there. Well, if we are dealing with four-hundred billion bits of information per second, yet we can only be consciously aware of two-thousand bits of information, and we decide to take up that relatively small amount by focussing on what we shouldn't be doing—isn't it highly likely that we are going to end up doing what we are focussing on?

Anyway, after the instructor released the group so that they could practice some more, he came over to me and said:

> "Sorry about that. Some of these people are just stupid. How many times do you have to tell them what they shouldn't do before they get it right?"

Well the answer to this question is never. If you don't want someone to contemplate something, don't mention it. There is no such thing as a negative instruction, comment, command or statement, as far as the mind is concerned. For the mind to consider what it shouldn't do it must first consider what it should do and then negate it, so 'Don't drop that' becomes 'Drop that—don't.' 'Don't do that' becomes 'Do that—don't,' and so on.

How may policies do you have at work that are biased towards what staff shouldn't do, as opposed to what they should do? And on top of that, how many procedures are there in place to deal with staff that have done what they shouldn't have done?

If I asked you now to make a list of all of the things that you didn't like or want, most people would find that easy. However, by doing that you will end up attracting more of the things you don't like or want into your conscious awareness and very possibly begin experiencing them.

Let me give you the example of a woman who came to me for therapy. Her 'problem' was that she could never find the right man to have a relationship with. As far as she was concerned, all men were bad. Every man she had ever been in a relationship with had treated her badly. I asked her to make a list of all of the things that she was looking for in a relationship with her ideal man. Ten minutes later I checked to see how she was doing. She had made a list, but it was a list of all of the things that she wasn't looking for in a relationship or with a man. It listed things like: "I don't want someone who . . . ," "I don't want a man to be . . . ," "I don't want to feel like I am . . ." and so on. I then asked her if the majority of the men that she had been in relationships with had treated her or made her feel the way she had listed to which she replied: *"Yes, nearly everyone I meet is the same. Why do I always attract the same type of man with the same type of problems? Why do they all seem to treat me as badly as the man before them did?"* When I explained to her about how our minds work she eventually got it, and then I asked her to make a list of all the things that she was looking for in a man—not the things she wasn't.

Now to many people this might sound a small, seemingly irrelevant thing to do, but it is actually one of the most important. As you will see, as you read further on, little changes, over time make for big changes overall. So just becoming aware and paying attention to the little things that we do and say is very important. By doing this we can make small regular changes, which over time will add up.

DOES THAT MEAN THAT IT'S NOT OK TO THINK ABOUT WHAT I DON'T WANT?

Of course not, provided you use it as a means of working towards what you do want and not as a means for justifying doing nothing. I think about what I don't want and that's fine. It gives me contrast and calibration in how I decide what I do want. Let me give you an example. Recently I asked a web-designer to design me a new website. I gave him a rough outline of what I wanted and pointed him towards some websites that I liked. As I am not a web designer, I can't get too involved with the small specific details, so I gave the designer a rough concept and some examples of what I wanted. However, neither the designer nor I knew exactly what I wanted right at the start.

When I received the first draft from him, I wasn't at all happy. It was certainly something I didn't want and I felt quite strongly about that. However, I still wasn't clear on what I specifically wanted. So what I did was focus on the bits of the design I really didn't like and explained that to the designer. In doing so I was able to use what I didn't like as contrast to put me on track to what I did want. In other words seeing what I didn't like made what I wanted slightly clearer to me and I was able to give him a bit of feedback on what I wanted to see. When I received the second draft it was better than the first, but it still wasn't right. So I explained to the designer the bits I liked, the bits I didn't, and again, provided him with a bit more specific detail about what I wanted. What was happening was I was able to provide more detailed feedback about what I wanted in contrast to what I didn't want in the drafts that he sent me. Eventually I ended up with a website that looks the way I want it to look based on deciding what I didn't want from the initial designs sent to me.

The key is that if you think about something you don't want, use it to work towards something you do want, even if you are not a hundred percent sure what it is that you want straight off. In one audio programme I recently listened to, entitled *The Secret*, they used the analogy of driving a car at night with the headlights on. What the speaker said was that the headlights only allow the driver to see about two hundred yards ahead, but that is enough to get you where you want to go. So provided we aim in the right direction and we continually modify and correct ourselves regularly, by monitoring the feedback we get, we can end up exactly where we want to be or with what we want.

So it's fine to focus on what you don't want, provided that you use it to drive you towards what you do want.

Look at the exercise below and have a go at reframing the negative statement in the left column to one that has a more positive aspect to it in the right column. By doing that we can train our minds to begin to focus in a more productive and effective way.

EXERCISE: REFRAMING EVERYDAY STATEMENTS

Statement / Question	New Reframed Positive Statement
Don't drop that!	Be careful.
I don't want to …	
The aspect of my job that I don't like is …	
I don't like …	

CHAPTER 3.
BODY LANGUAGE—
YOUR BODY BELIEVES
EVERY WORD YOU SAY

"You must be the change you want to see in the world."
Mahatma Gandhi

We have more neurons (the electrically excitable cells that process and transmit information) in our brains than there are stars and planets in the known galaxies.

Our physical bodies are made up of trillions of cells, fifty trillion to be precise, a cell being the smallest structural and functional unit of all known living organisms and which are sometimes referred to as the building blocks of life.

Our cells carry out an amazing variety of functions. For example, they manage our digestive system, control our respiratory system, enable our bodies to fight viruses and disease, regulate body temperature and orchestrate muscle movement. We also now know that each cell has a tiny director sitting inside of its centre known as DNA. This director, or DNA, is identical in every cell, whether it is a brain cell, blood cell or bone cell.

What is amazing is that all of the cells in one person's body grew out of one double strand of DNA at the moment of conception. The colour of our eyes, the shape of our distinctive family nose down through the generations, our physical posture and everything we can do—for example, think, speak, run, play the guitar, heal a cut, run a successful company or nation, builds on a capacity present in that one original molecule of DNA.

In short DNA is a set of coded instructions that determine our genetic make-up. It is similar to an architect's plan for a house. But is it set in stone? Is our destiny affected and determined by our DNA, or can our DNA be influenced by the way we think and the choices we make?

In addition to DNA, each and every cell has hundreds of receptors on it's surface, designed to take in information, and each and every cell can, at the direction of its DNA, send out messengers by way of the chemicals it produces to every other cell in the body. What this means is that every cell in our body has the ability to communicate with every other cell. In essence, each cell has it's own consciousness and recent breakthroughs in physics and biology have revealed to us is that the body is full of intelligence.

EMOTIONAL ADDICTION

Candice Pert is a doctor who has undertaken empirical research into how our cells communicate. What she discovered was that the cells of our body have receptors on their surface called '*neuro-receptors.*' She states that each cell has literally thousands of these receptors on its surface, which is know as the membrane.

In the brain there is a part known as the *hypothalamus* which is the largest natural drug-manufacturing pharmaceutical company in the world. The hypothalamus produces chemicals called *neuropeptides*, which are chains of amino acids, in response to our emotional states. So we have chemicals for anger, chemicals for love, chemicals for depression, chemicals for happiness, and so on. In short, every emotional state we experience has its roots in an amino acid chain called a *neuropeptide*. Once produced by the hypothalamus, these neuropeptides flood though our body and interact with every cell in it. Candice Pert actually refers to these neuropeptides as *"bits of brain floating through the body."*

When these neuropeptides reach a cell what they do is 'dock' with the receptors on the cells surface. In essence the neuropeptide acts as a key that fits into the neuroreceptor acting like a lock, stimulating the cell into action and changing the chemical make up of the cell.

Over time a cell that has been consistently stimulated by a particular strand of neuropeptide will crave more of the same drug (neuropeptide). In short the cell generates a memory of what it wants and communicates back to the brain to send it more. In short, we can create a closed feedback loop that is almost like an addictive state.

This is why, over time, angry people find it easier to become angry, depressed people find it easier to become more depressed and happy people find it easier to be happy. In short they find more reasons to self-satisfy the emotional cravings that they have created through distorted thinking. In essence, they have become nothing more than addicted to their own emotional states.

Each and every one of our fifty-trillion cells thinks and communicates with each other, and are using the same chemical (neuropeptides) to do so. In fact, each cell in the body has a mind of its own, and has its own independent intelligence and consciousness.

THE INTERNAL DRUG COMPANY

One important aspect of the mind and body's intelligence is its ability to create a wide variety of natural drugs. For example, when you are feeling calm your body is producing it's own version of Valium. When we are feeling brave or invincible, our bodies are making a neuropeptide similar to interleukin-2; one of the most powerful and effective chemicals used to fight cancer cells. When we feel happy our bodies are flooded with *endorphins,* chemicals that enhance our sense of pleasure and well-being, and which also boost our immune system helping us to resist and fight off bacteria and viruses. What is fundamentally brilliant is that all of these 'natural drugs' are produced by our bodies, in exactly the right quantity and targeted exactly at the right cells. In essence our bodies seem to know what we need and where we need it—without any of the side effects that are common with many synthetic drugs made by pharmaceutical companies.

So if I were to decide to dive off of a high board at the swimming pool and I felt excited at the though of it, I would be producing neuropeptides such as interlukin-2. However, if in the same situation I was dreading the thought of it, I would be producing stress hormones such as cortisol and adrenaline. In short, our thoughts affect our cells. Happy thoughts become happy cells and unhappy thoughts become unhappy cells.

YOU'RE JUST A LOAD OF EMPTY SPACE

Our cells are, in turn, made of atoms (hydrogen, carbon, oxygen, etc) that make up our cellular, organic and skeletal structures. To give you some idea of the size of an atom—one million carbon atoms could fit across a human hair. Also, consider this, there are more atoms in a standard glass of water than there are glasses of water in all of the oceans of the world! It is also a fact that 99.9% of an atom is empty space, with electrons orbiting a small nucleus made up of positively charged neutrons and protons. The nucleus of an atom is so small that if it were the size of a football the nearest orbiting electron would be a half a mile away.

So, if we are made up of atoms, that means is that we are 99.9% empty space. Now, try to understand this. If all the empty space were sucked out of the atoms in your body right now, you would shrink down to nothing more than the size of a grain of salt. If we did this to the entire human race, what we would be left with would fit inside an apple!

According to current scientific evidence, most of the atoms in the human body were made just a few minutes after the birth of the universe. As a result we have the same atoms in us as does a tree, a blade of grass, the bricks that make the buildings we live and work in, the chairs we sit on and the beds we sleep in.

In addition, we replace ninety-eight percent of the atoms that compose our body once a year. Not a single cell that existed in your body in 2002 or 2006 exists in it today. We also change our skin once a month and our liver is new every six weeks. The brain cells that we think with, the actual carbon, hydrogen, nitrogen and oxygen molecules that made it up a year ago are not there any more. Even the DNA molecules inside every cell (the carbon, hydrogen oxygen molecules that make up the DNA) weren't there three or four months ago. As Deepak Chopra says in his book *Quantum Healing*[4]:

> *It is as if you lived in a building whose bricks were systematically taken out and replaced every year. If you kept the*

---

4. *Quantum Healing* by Deepak Chopra, .M.D., Bantam Books (1989), ISBN 0-553-17332-4.

same blueprint [DNA], then it will still look like the same building. But it won't be the same in actuality. The human body also stands there looking much the same from day to day, but through the process of respiration, digestion, elimination and so forth, it is constantly and ever in exchange with the rest of the world.

In essence we are forever changing. Every part of our being is re-created and replaced on a regular basis, and how we choose to feel dictates what chemicals we produce that affect that process. We are a quantum being that exists within the infinite void of unlimited and potential possibility that is us. We have the capacity and resources to become whatever we chose to become. We are not tethered by the past. Our futures are not pre-determined. We are free to be who and what we want to be. As Muhammad Ali, who in my opinion is not only possibly the greatest boxer that ever lived, but also a great philosopher and humanitarian said:

> "I know where I'm going and I know the truth and I don't have to be what you want me to be. I'm free to be what I want."

YOUR PAST IS NOT YOUR FUTURE

Bruce H. Lipton is an internationally recognised authority on cell biology. In his book, *The Biology of Belief*[5], he states that cell biologists used to believe that the nucleus of a cell was the cell's brain because that was where the DNA is stored. However, in experiments where the nucleus of a cell was removed the cell still managed to live on and survive for up to two or more months without its 'brain' in place. The reason these cells eventually die is not because they have lost their brain *per se*, but because they have lost the ability to reproduce.

A new emergent field in biology, known as *Epigenetics* (meaning 'control above genetics'), has established that DNA blue

---

5. *The Biology of Belief* by Bruce H. Lipton, Mountain of Love (2005), ISBN 0-9759914-7-7.

prints passed down through our genes are not set in concrete at birth. In short our genes are not our destiny. Epigenetic research has shown that other factors such as environmental influences, nutrition, stress and emotions all serve to modify our genes, without changing their basic blueprint. It also showed that these modifications could be passed on to future generations.

Now, this is groundbreaking research. What it proves is extremely important. It shows that many things that we take as being heredity, are not.

In essence our past does not necessarily dictate our future!

For example, studies have found that only 5% of cancer and cardiovascular patients can attribute their disease to hereditary factors. However, what is not emphasised, according to Lipton and the epigenetic research, is that ninety-five percent of breast cancers are not due to inherited genes. The malignancies in a significant number of cancer patients are derived from environmentally induced epigenetic alterations and not defective genes.

Furthermore, in recent years cell biologists have gained even more insight into the amazing abilities of the membrane (the outer layer) of our cells. What they have shown is that the cell membrane digests, breathes, excretes waste matter and even exhibits *neurological processing*. These single cells can also sense where there is food and move themselves towards it! Similarly, a single cell can also recognise toxins and predators, and purposely employ escape manoeuvres to save their lives. In other words, every cell displays intelligence.

Lipton's work on cell membranes led him to define and describe the membrane as follows:

> "The membrane is a liquid crystal semiconductor with gates and channels."

This led him into a fascinating paradox when he read the definition of a computer chip as being: *"A chip is a crystal semiconductor with gates and channels."* In short, a cell membrane is a structural and functional equivalent of a silicone chip. This led him to realise two things:

1. That computers and cells are *programmable*, and
2. The *programmer* lies *outside* the computer and the cell.

In other words biological behaviour and gene activity are dynamically linked to information from the environment, which is subsequently downloaded into the cell.

Lipton began to realise that the nucleus of a cell is simply a memory disc, like a computer hard drive, containing the DNA programmes that encode the production of proteins and data that is entered into the cell via the membrane's receptors, which he likened to a computer keyboard (the cells membrane) entering data into a computer (the cell's nucleus).

Lipton concludes that '*a cell's operations are primarily moulded by its interaction with the environment, not by its genetic code.*' This is not to dispute that DNA is not remarkable in itself. DNA has evolved over millions and possibly billions of years, but as remarkable as DNA is, it does not "control" the operations of our cells.

THE EFFECT OF THE ENVIRONMENT

In short, the environment is without doubt the main programmable factor in how cells change and develop. Now, this is not necessarily new thinking. The great English naturalist and geologist, Charles Darwin, whose book *The Origin of Species* published in 1859, provided scientific evidence to show that animals and plants changed over time dependent on their natural environment. His findings were driven by his need to explain why there were so many different varieties within the same species. His conclusions showed that through the process of natural selection those species and plants that adapted better, and that had the ability to change more readily to their ever changing environment, would subsequently have a greater chance of surviving and passing on their genes to future generations.

For example, many of you who watched the 2008 Beijing Olympics would have been mesmerized by Usain Bolt, the 21 year-old Jamaican sprinter who smashed the 100 and 200 metre World and Olympic records to win Gold in both races. He was also in the winning 4 x 100m relay team, giving him a total of three Olympic Gold medals overall. His amazing conquests, and the speed at which he carried them out, have marked him out as the greatest sprinter in human evolutionary history. In addition to Bolt, other Jamaica runners were also breaking records. The first three runners over the line in the 100 metre Olympic final were all Jamaican. This was the first clean sweep of its kind in this event in either a World or Olympic Championship, and another Jamaican athlete, Melanie Walker, won Gold in the 400 metre hurdles setting a new Olympic record in the process.

So what makes the great Jamaicans so great? Is it nature or is it nurture? In other words, are they born that way or is it something they acquire? To answer this we need to look closer at the culture which produces these great athletes.

Jamaican culture evolves around sport and there is a national system in place to help young people develop their sporting talent. It starts with Jamaican schools that take athletics and sport very seriously. They even have sporting talent scouts whose job it is to track down and identify talented children and then talk to the parents to try and convince them to send their children to their schools. Every year at Jamaica's national sports stadium thirty-thousand cheering fans can be seen supporting their school friends who are competing in the events. This national amateur school event draws a larger crowd of supporters each year than most European, Commonwealth and International athletic events. In addition, all around the national stadium, there is a hall of fame where all of the great Jamaican sports men and women have their portraits on public display for all to see. This encourages the young competitors to want to emulate their great sporting heroes.

What is happening in Jamaica is that biology is being affected directly by environment. In this case in a culture that nurtures and supports its athletes from a very early age. This structure is unique to Jamaica and doesn't exist anywhere else in the world. Is it any wonder, therefore, that Jamaica produces some of the world's greatest sprinters and athletes.

With regard to the environment of the cell, the most influential factor that will affect it, based on Lipton's research, has to be the way we think. Negative thoughts will produce negative chemicals and toxins that flood our system and interact with every cell in our body. These thoughts, if generated consistently over time, will, according to epigenetic research and Lipton's findings, undoubtedly affect the cell. As all of our organs are made up of cells, negative or destructive thinking which affects every cell, will end up affecting our bodily organs.

However, if that is true of negative thoughts, it must also hold true of positive thoughts also. Positive thoughts and being happy will generate positive chemicals in our system which will provide good protein sources for our cells to live and thrive in, which over time, will have a more positive and beneficial effect on our health and well-being.

In short we are in control of our lives and not, as Lipton puts it *"in the genetic roll of the dice at conception."* Lipton goes on to state: *"We are the drivers of our own biology, just as I am the driver of this word processing programme. We have the ability to edit the data we enter into our bio-computers, just as surely as I can choose the words I type."*

Earlier we stated that we replace ninety-eight percent of the atoms that compose our body once a year, and that all of our cells are constantly ebbing and flowing in and out of existence. In short, the cells we have now were not there last year. Therefore, when surgeons and doctors look at an x-ray of a cancer tumour that was initially diagnosed several months earlier they are not looking at the same tumour. All of the diseased cells that made up that tumour have been replaced. In short the cancer they now see is a new cancer that has simply repeated the pattern of existence set earlier on.

We also regularly hear of individuals who have been diagnosed with life-threatening illnesses—and have had no medical intervention, who in contrast to the prognosis, recover from the illness when such a recovery should not be possible. This is normally referred to as a 'miracle cure' or a 'spontaneous remission,' inferring that this is an exception to the general rule. In short, the scientific and medical community has no way of understanding or explaining why such a remission should occur. Therefore, the remission is put down to luck!

However, if these spontaneous cures can (and do) occur, even if only in a small minority of cases, this tells people like Dr. Chopra and Dr. Lipton that each of us is could be capable of it. In short,

Dr. Chopra explains in his book, *Quantum Healing*, that every day a few cancer cells arise in our bodies and automatically the DNA in the body's cells knows how to rid us of them. He states that a spontaneous remission is only an exaggerated phenomenon of what is happening all of the time in each and every one of us.

One of the very interesting points Dr. Chopra makes in his book is that memory is possibly more important than matter. For example, whilst our skin cells change once a month they don't forget the difference between hot and cold. The cells that make up our taste buds change all of the time but they don't forget the difference between sweet and sour. The cells of our DNA change as atoms every three months, but they seem to remember the whole history of our evolution up to this point in time. DNA therefore, according to Dr. Chopra, is more memory than matter. Every time we encounter a disease or illness our DNA remembers the first time such a disease was encountered by the human race. He explains that it is actually these memories contained within the DNA that reincarnate themselves as the molecules of our bodies.

Now what Dr. Chopra is referring to is very important. If we have understood the dynamics of quantum mechanics in terms of how our sub-atomic particles regenerate themselves on an ongoing and regular basis then we have to accept that the atoms that actually composed the initial cancer are not only long gone, but simply no longer there. It is in fact a new cancer that is being viewed six months later composed of entirely new atoms.

What is happening is that the person who had the cancer is recreating the cancer time and time again. Now physicists can destroy the cancer down to the last cell with chemotherapy, radiation treatment and surgery, but what Dr. Chopra is saying is:

> "Unless one deals with the distorted patterns of intelligence that structure the physical expression of that cancer, unless we 'exorcise' the ghost of the cancer the cancer will keep reappearing. This is because the cancer itself is not just the molecules that make it up, it is the distorted pattern of intelligence that have led to the physical manifestation of the cancerous cells."

Now this holds true for any disease as well as for any perception of reality. For example, if we believe that stress is an illness (which it is not!) and that we are 'always stressed' then we will produce the thinking that will lead to stress-related illnesses. Because we can imagine and envisage these illnesses, it is also possible that someone can make us believe that we can get them as well.

Therefore, if we hold distorted patterns of thinking as being true—then we will produce distorted patterns of behaviour to support the thinking. We will do this not only at the macroscopic level, but also at the microscopic, cellular and subatomic levels.

However, the converse also must hold true. If we generate more functional patterns of thinking, then we can create a more positive environment for our cells to thrive in. We have the power and the ability to tap into an unlimited expanse of universal potential by simply changing the way we think, and, possibly more importantly, the way we think abut the way we think.

One simple fact remains. The more happier and content you are, the more positive you are, then the healthier you are and will become. Healthy thinking = healthy body.

CHAPTER 4.
THE GROOVE THEORY OF HABITUAL BEHAVIOUR

How do you make yourself happy? Simple! Have happy thoughts. How do you bring more pleasure and joy into your life? Simple! Focus on what brings you more pleasure and joy, and not on what doesn't. Now at this stage that might all sound too simplistic to be true, and many delegates who attend my training courses regularly say *"It can't be that simple, can it?"* Well the truth is it can, but the reality is that if you want something different in your life—if you want more joy, more happiness, more financial wealth, better health and well-being—you have to start thinking differently and you have to do it regularly. This chapter is about just those things.

Think about it this way; if you were going shopping, would you go with a list of all the things you didn't want, or of all the things you did want? Obviously, you would make a list of all of the things you were going shopping for so that you wouldn't forget them, as they are things you want. It would seem odd to say to your partner *"Oh honey, don't forget not to buy some milk, we don't need it!"*

Yet when it comes to what we want out of our lives many people focus on what they don't want as opposed to what they ***do*** want! The reality is however, that what we focus on we get more of, and so by constantly thinking about what we don't want, we actually end up attracting it into our lives!

In an experiment done in 1953, the graduating class of Harvard University was asked if they had a written list for what they wanted in life, and an action plan for carrying it out. Out of the whole graduating class that year only 3% had a written list of goals, along with action plans for making those goals a reality. Twenty years later in 1973 the same graduating class was contacted by the researchers who undertook the initial experiment in 1953. What they found was that the 3% who had written goals, and an action plan had greater financial wealth, and better health and well-being than the remaining 97% combined!

How many people do you know that consistently moan about their financial situation, their relationships, or their health? How many of those people actually find it easier to moan about their situation because things always seem to go wrong for them? Doesn't it almost seem like they give into or cause these bad things to happen in order for them to prove their own sad theories about themselves?

The fundamental fact is that our thoughts govern our behaviour, and the more we think in a certain way the more we will continue to think in that same way again. We produce habits in our patterns of thought.

A habit is basically something that we do without thinking or being aware of it. We can be fooled into believing that because we didn't think about it—it's not our fault. The fact actually is that for us to be able to do something without thinking we must have at some time in the past had to conceive of it, apply our mind to it—or otherwise we would never have learned *how* to do it in the first place.

For example, think of the first time you had to learn a new skill—like riding a bike or perfecting a martial arts move, or giving a new presentation or adopting a new position at work. In the early stages of each of these examples you had to apply your mind and focus your attention on what you wanted to perfect, until you were happy with the outcome. Once happy with the outcome, you stopped consciously having to think about it.

Habits are merely patterns that occur in our thinking and in our behaviour. In short they are 'mental grooves' that the needle of our thinking falls into without us having to think about it.

Here is a fact, every time you think or behave in a certain way you increase the probability that you will think or behave in that way again. In a book called *The Inner Game of Tennis*[6] by W. Timothy Gallwey this phenomena is explained excellently:

---

6. *The Inner Game of Tennis* by W. Timothy Gallwey, Pan Books (1986), ISBN 0-330-29513-6.

> *One hears a lot of talk about grooving one's strokes in tennis. The theory is a simple one: every time you swing your racket in a certain way, you increase the probabilities that you will swing that way again. In this way patterns, called grooves, build up which have a predisposition to repeat themselves. It is as if the nervous system were like a record disc. Every time an action is performed, a slight impression is made in the microscopic cells of the brain, just as a leaf blowing over a fine-grained beach of sand will leave its faint trace. When the same action is repeated, the groove is made slightly deeper. After many similar actions there is a more recognisable groove into which the needle of behaviour seems to fall automatically.*

Habits are statements about the past, so by acting without thinking we are simply reliving the past every day. This is OK if we like what we are doing, or if we are enjoying our life—but what if we don't? What if we don't like the reality of the way we are living our life? What if we don't enjoy being depressed or stressed? What if we want to change the fact that we are too quick to anger?

Many of you will know how hard it can be to fight your way out of a deep mental groove and this is possibly why some 'non-directive talk therapies' simply don't work. The fact is that if you spend time talking or focusing on the very behaviour that you don't like, you actually help to create a deeper groove (You get more of what you focus on).

Well there is a simpler solution—just change the way you think. In other words, 'cut yourself a new groove!'

NEURONS THAT FIRE TOGETHER, WIRE TOGETHER.

Now this may sound simple, but there is a neurological law called 'Hebb's Law' that states that neurons *"that fire together wire together."* What that means is that the more we think a certain way, the more we will strengthen the neurological connections that deepen that particular groove, linking the cells in the mind that allow us to think that way without thinking. In this way habitual behaviour is born.

> "When two elementary brain processes have been active together in immediate succession, one of them, on reoccurring, tends to propagate its excitement into the other."
>
> William James, the Father of American Psychology, 1890

Neural connections in our brains are continually being sculpted by the way we think and the way we act. One research study that illustrated this fact was where researchers looked at the brains of deceased people. What they found was that the cells in the brain areas of typists and machine operators were more developed when compared with other areas of the brain devoted to less frequent activity. They also found something else even more remarkable. In post-mortem examinations of the brains of a number of people of differing ages, they found that those individuals who had undertaken more education during heir lifetime had actually physically recruited more neurons into the areas of their brains dedicated to language, resulting in a lager neural networks in these areas of the brain.

Research has also shown that the brain areas dedicated to the fingers of blind people who use Braille are also enlarged. This has also been proved for the fingers of musicians such as violinists and cellists, who, after years of practice, have developed larger neural-networks of dedicated neurons devoted to their skill, honed by years of practice. What this proves is that the more we do something the more we increase the neural activity dedicated to what we do. The more active the neurons associated with the activity become, the more they recruit more neurons into play to increase the size of the neural network associated with the activity.

USING THE MENTAL GYM

But what about thought? Athletes not only train on the track, they also train in the mind, the mental gym. Steve Backley[7] is a British javelin-thrower and Olympic medalist. On one occasion Backley sprained his ankle four-weeks before the competitive season began, resulting in him being immobile for two weeks. Now this is a major disadvantage for an athlete at this stage of the season. What Backley did was use his mind, the greatest virtual reality generator in the universe. He imagined himself throwing the javelin in every major stadium in the world. He mentally rehearsed his technique—which at first, he found difficult because he found it hard to visualise his mental throws without his ankle making him limp. However, he found that if he concentrated his mental imagery on his good leg, he could visualise perfect throws. As a result when his ankle got better, he was able to resume training, carrying on right from where he left off before he was injured with no detriment to his performance.

Scientific research has now proven that we can take an athlete, and wire them up to sophisticated biofeedback equipment whilst they are running on a treadmill to measure their mental and muscular activity. Then, at some time later, we can then take the same athlete, wire them up to the same bio-feedback equipment, sit them in a chair and get them to visualise themselves running on the treadmill. What is phenomenal is that we get the same biofeedback results from the visualization as we do from the actual event itself. What this proves is that the brain does not know the difference between what is going on in its environment and what is going on in the mind. This is because when we imagine ourselves doing something the neurological responses produced by our brains are the same as they would be if we were actually doing it.

In another experiment researchers got people to learn a one-handed five-finger exercise on the piano. They were made to practice the exercise for two hours a day for five days. At the end the brain scans showed that the neural networks of the area of the brain dedicated to this exercise actually got bigger. But here's the

---

7. *The Winning Mind: A Guide to Achieving Success and Overcoming Failure* by Steve Backley and Ian Stafford, Aurum Press Ltd (2000), ISBN: 978-1854104045.

really interesting part. Another group was instructed to carry out the same exercise, but only by using metal imagery and visualization. The outcome was that this group showed very similar changes in the neural networks of their brains to that of the group who actually undertook the physical practice. In other words, they increased the size of the neural network in the areas of their brains dedicated to this exercise purely by using thought.[8]

MONKEY SEE—MONKEY DO

The discovery of mirror neurons is possibly the single most important finding of the decade, and might possibly do for psychology what DNA did for biology. Mirror neurons help explain how we learn through observation, which is an important aspect for us to understand if, for example, we are to instruct others in a physical skill.

Mirror neurons are brain cells which are predominately found in the frontal lobes. Earlier studies with monkeys revealed that mirror neurons respond both when we do something and also when we simply watch someone else do it. Although it was initially known that these neurons fire when we performed an action, it came as quite a surprise that the same cells also fired when we only saw that action being performed.

In a more recent study undertaken by researchers at the University of College London, dancers from London's Royal Ballet and experts in Capoeira, a Brazilian martial art, were asked to watch short videos of either ballet or Capoeira dancers performing brief dance moves. While watching the videos, the dancers were lying perfectly still on in an MRI scanner. What the researchers found was that areas of the brain collectively known as the "mirror neuron system" showed more activity when a dancer saw movement they had been trained to perform than when they observed movements they hadn't been trained to perform.

The evidence suggests that anytime you watch someone else doing something (or even starting to do something), the corre

---

[8]. *Mind Sculpture* by Ian Robertson, Bantam Books Ltd (2000), ISBN: 0-553-81325-0.

sponding mirror neurons fire in your brain, thus aiding recall through recognition. As Daniel Glaser, a neuroscientist who was part of the UCL team stated: *"This is the first proof that your personal motor repertoire, the things that you yourself have learned to do, changes the way that your brain responds when you see movement."*

The findings of the UCL researchers suggest that once the brain has learned a skill it continues to stimulate the development of the skill through the process of observation or visualisation of it.

USE IT OR LOSE IT!

However, there is also another statement of fact promoted by this Hebbian Law, and that is: *"use it or lose it—neurons that fire apart wire apart."* In essence the less we think in a certain way the more likely we are to break the habit.

Therefore, if you want to stop feeling sad—stop thinking sad thoughts and replace them with happy ones. If we do this then the 'groove' made by the habitual sad thinking is weakened and the groove made by the new happy thinking becomes more entrenched.

Imagine that outside your work building is a beautiful square patch of grass that is pristine and well kept, like a bowling green. On the other side of the grass is a really good café or restaurant where most people go for their lunch. In the middle of the patch of grass there is a sign saying 'Keep off the Grass' and most self-respecting people do just that. They take the time to walk around it to go to the café. One day however, the sky opens and it begins to pour with rain. It is lunchtime and people are running around the grass to get to the café. However, one person, not wanting to get soaking wet, ignores the sign and runs across the grass, leaving faint footprints. As they do so other people notice that no-one has enforced the 'Keep off the Grass' warning, and so the person is not reprimanded for running across the grass. As a result, other people, also not wishing to get wet, run across the grass too, using it as a short cut to the café. And, as more and more people walk or run across the grass, their combined footprints leave a muddy, yet well recognisable path across the grass. Over time that walkway would become a natural pathway as the grass stops growing where people have been walking over it.

Now lets imagine that the Queen, who one morning passes by it in her car on her way to the Palace, owns the patch of grass. On seeing the sorry state of the grass she stops the car and inspects further. Dismayed that people have been so inconsiderate she orders that another sign is erected that says: '*Walk on the Grass and you will be Shot.*' The Queen also orders that an armed soldier with Crown immunity to shoot and kill anyone who walks on the grass be placed there permanently to stop anyone else from walking on it. Now that should be enough motivation to stop anyone from wanting to walk on the grass don't you think? So as people revert back to walking around the grass and not on it what do you think will eventually happen to the grass over time? Obviously it would revert back to what it looked like before, a beautiful, well-kept, pristine square patch of natural grass.

Be mindful of where you tread with regard to your thinking. Every thought leaves faint footprints in our minds that can become the pathways of habitual behaviour through repetition along the same path. Choose your path carefully, decide which road best serves your interests and well-being. Just because something is well trodden doesn't mean it's the best way. Sometimes it's best to use the road less travelled.

The Road Less Travelled

Two roads diverged in a yellow wood,
And sorry I could not travel both
And be one traveller, long I stood
And looked down one as far as I could
To where it bent in the undergrowth.

Then took the other, as just as fair,
And having perhaps the better claim,
Because it was grassy and wanted wear;
Though as for that the passing there
Had worn them really about the same.

And both that morning equally lay
In leaves no step had trodden black.
Oh, I kept the first for another day!
Yet knowing how way leads on to way,
I doubted if I should ever come back.

I shall be telling this with a sigh
Somewhere ages and ages hence:
Two roads diverged in a wood, and I -
I took the one less travelled by,
And that has made all the difference.

Robert Frost

BIRDS OF A FEATHER FLOCK TOGETHER—LIKE ATTRACTS LIKE

You may be surprised to know that the neural networks of our brains that create our everyday reality work in much the same way. By choosing how you focus your thoughts, you can choose how you design or change your life for the better. If you want to create more financial wealth in your life, start focusing on what you have, not what you don't have. If you want better health in your life start focusing on how healthy you are, not what's wrong with you. If you want better relationships with others, focus on what's good about those you interact with, focus on what they do right, not what they do wrong. It really is that simple, but it needs to be done on a regular and consistent basis.

REPETITION IS THE MOTHER OF ALL CHANGE

Think about it, if you want to get big biceps you need to go to a gym—more than once! If you want to lose weight you need to eat the right foods and do the right exercise—regularly—not once. If you want to think more constructively then you need to do it regularly, and I would suggest that you do a little every day. Spend fifteen to thirty minutes a day sitting—or lying in a quiet place and focus your mind on what you want to achieve—not what you don't want. Using again the analogy of lifting weights or going down to the gym, the hardest part is actually making the commitment to go. Once you start then you go slowly at first. You lift light weights, or run for a few minutes at a slow pace. It feels unnatural or uncomfortable at first, you are conscious of others looking at you and you may even feel embarrassed. Yet it is the very act of commitment, the ability to work through it with an end-goal in mind, that makes the sweat and strain bearable and ultimately results in an increased level of fitness and strength. This training is no different. It needs to be done regularly and you need to start at the beginning. It will feel odd, and you may not feel totally comfortable with it, but over time it will become a habit, but a more functional one, and once you have started creating a more functional groove, other less functional grooves will be used less, and neurons that aren't used are lost!

CAPTAIN JACK SPARROW'S COMPASS: 'WHERE DO YOU MOST WANT TO GO?'

Many of you will have seen the film *The Pirates of the Caribbean: Dead Man's Chest* starring Johnny Depp as 'Captain Jack Sparrow,' Kiera Knightly as 'Elizabeth Swann,' and Orlando Bloom as 'Will Turner.'

Throughout both films, Captain Jack Sparrow regularly checks his trusty compass without much luck. The compass needle seems to oscillate aimlessly, the result of which is that the compass never seems to take him where he wants to go.

In the second film, *Dead Man's Chest*, Will Turner finds himself onboard the ghost ship under the command of Davy Jones. At one point in the film Elizabeth Swann asks Captain Jack Sparrow to help her find Will, her true love. In response Captain Jack hands her the compass and tells her that the compass will only ever point to where you really want to go. As she holds the compass in her hand and wishes to be re-united with Will, the compass needle directs Elizabeth on the true course that she needs to follow to find her love.

The compass, it seems, will only ever point you towards what you really, really want to move towards. As Captain Jack Sparrow is forever evading someone or something, the compass cannot point in the direction that he really wants to go because his motivation seemingly is governed by the need for him to be always avoiding someone or something. Elizabeth, on the other hand, is motivated by the need to move towards something that she really, really wants—her true love Will, so the compass works for her.

THE MIRROR OF ERISED

A similar set of conditions can be found in the Harry Potter books (by J.K. Rowling) and films. In one of the films, there is a mirror called *The Mirror of Erised*, that will only show you what you want most of all in the world. When Harry looks in the mirror he can see his parents when others only see there own reflections.

On the mirror there is an inscription which reads: 'ERISED STRA EHRU OYT UBE CAFRU OYT ON WOHSI'—which, when read backwards reads: "I SHOW NOT YOUR FACE BUT YOUR HEART'S DESIRE." According to Dumbledore (the Headmaster of the school), the Mirror *"shows us nothing more or less than the deepest, most desperate desire of our hearts."*

Therefore, when Harry looks in the mirror he sees what his heart desires most—his parents. Those others who look in the mirror and see nothing except their reflection are possibly only dealing with the world as it presents itself to them, not as they would have it presented.

Recently I was running a course on NLP, when one of the delegates took great delight in informing me that 'none of this mumbo-jumbo actually works' (he was right of course—regarding himself). His conclusion was based on the fact that he had bought and read some self-help books in the past, but they were *"obviously rubbish"* because they didn't work—for him. When I asked him which books he had purchased, he couldn't tell me. After some more probing questions, he confessed that he had only read the first couple of chapters and then discarded the book because he didn't agree with it. I asked him whether or not he actually believed that the books could make a positive difference in his life, to which he replied, *"No, not really."* To cut a long story short, he paid money for something that he didn't believe would work and that he didn't even read through to the end. Therefore, he is right in his assumption that it doesn't work. Interestingly enough, recent research has now shown that reading self-help or self-improvement books are actually better than taking anti-depressants—unless of course, you believe that it's not true!

On another occasion, I was informed by a lady that hypnosis was *"a load of old rubbish."* She had gone to a hypnotherapist to stop smoking, and after a number of visits, she still hadn't managed to give up the habit.

"He was very good," she said, *"he tried everything to get me to stop, but I knew he was wasting his time. That hypnosis stuff is a load of old rubbish."* "Did you want to stop smoking?" I asked her. "Of course," she replied. "No, you misunderstand me," I continued, "did you really, really want to stop smoking?" "Not really," she replied, "but I thought I'd give it a go as my friend said it had worked for her."

These examples illustrate the power of belief, which is something we will look into in the next chapter.

We have had many clues throughout the evolution of humankind as to the power of our minds and the power of belief. In the Bible (the best-selling book in history) Jesus says to his disciples, in the parable of the Fig Tree (*Mark 11.21*):

> I assure you that whoever tells this hill to get up and throw itself in the sea and does not doubt in his heart, but believes that what he says will happen, it will be done for him. For this reason I tell you: when you pray and ask for something, believe that you have received it, and you will be given whatever you ask for.

If you consider the world of quantum mechanics you will come across an argument that what we see is nothing more than the projection of whatever we believe to be there. Based upon the principle that our minds create our reality second by second, minute by minute, day by day what we see is nothing more than a representation of what we think exists, founded on the reality that we allow to materialize inside our minds. To illustrate this, someone created the film Pirates of the Caribbean from an idea that manifested itself inside their mind, an idea which many of us can now see as a projection of another person's vision—can't we?

Therefore, maybe Captain Jack Sparrow's Compass, the Mirror of Erised from the Harry Potter stories and the parables of the Bible have more to their meaning than can be seen on one level.

COUNT YOUR BLESSINGS

Professor Martin Seligman is a positive psychologist who has spent more than twenty years rigorously testing the effectiveness of various exercises, psychotherapies and drugs and the effect they have in combating depression to find out what works. In addition he has trained thousands of coaches, psychologists, parents and teachers in a wide range of exercises designed to improve positivity and happiness. His results have been, for many, life changing.

Seligman looked at the effect on severe depression of doing an exercise he entitled *'Three blessings,'* which basically consisted of simply writing down three things that went well each day and why. The results of this simple exercise were outstanding. What he found was that 94% of severely depressed people became less depressed and 92% became happier, with an average symptom relief of a whopping 50% over only 15 days. What was even more amazing was that when he compared his exercise with patients on prescribed medication he found that by the end of three months about 10% of the patients who were taking medication or treatment improved (as is normally expected), compared to a whopping 70% of the patients who used the three blessings as part of their positive psychotherapy intervention. As a direct result depressive symptoms were substantially reduced and happiness markedly increased.

What Seligman noticed was that not only did this type of exercise have positive benefits among relatively untroubled people; it also has a major positive impact for those individuals who were suffering from serious depression. One of the main conclusions he drew was that traditionally psychotherapy is where you go to talk about your troubles. Therefore, providing psychotherapeutic interventions where individuals are encouraged to focus on positive aspects of their lives is a much more functional approach.

DEVELOPING AN ATTITUDE OF GRATITUDE

A starting point for developing a happier outlook and to attract more of what we want into our lives is to become grateful for what we already have. Developing an 'attitude of gratitude' therefore, provides us with the opportunity to tune our conscious minds into a more positive focus by allowing us to notice the benefits that already exist in our lives.

As adults, fear, worry and anxiety can suppress and impede our ability for us to be grateful for what we have. However, the important factor to consider is does being grateful work?

Is taking the time to be grateful really worth it? Can it affect our lives in positive ways? Can it help reduce stress and anxiety and lead us towards a happier and more fulfilling life? Well, according to some solid new science, the answer is yes.

In a recent paper on chronic financial strain, Dr. Neal Krause, professor for Health Behaviour and Health Education at the University of Michigan, explored gratitude as a way of reducing and combating the negative effects of modern day stress.

Krause's work looked into the persistent financial problems that are commonly linked to depression in older people. His study was focussed on identifying factors that might alleviate those depressive symptoms, and the role gratitude plays in people coping with financial strain, and even how religion shapes a sense of gratitude.

According to his findings gratitude has significant stress-buffering potential in the midst of economic anxiety. Dr. Krause stated that while *"chronic financial strain has a fairly substantial impact on depressive symptoms for older adults who are relatively less grateful . . . the noxious effects of persistent economic problems on depressive symptoms are completely offset for older people who feel the most grateful."*

And gratitude doesn't just offer insurance against the stress of economic uncertainty. Krause's work also suggests that *"greater feelings of gratitude are associated with greater life satisfaction, greater happiness, and fewer symptoms of depression."*

Why does gratitude work this way? Well according to Krause it's because *"people with a greater sense of gratitude are more likely to ask for social support from significant others, find growth in the face of adversity, and engage in positive coping responses, such as active problem solving."*

His data also showed that those who attend worship services more frequently express more feelings of gratitude. As Krause and other researchers explain, individuals who believe God's purposes are at work in their lives see difficulty as a part of his plan and understand trials as opportunities for spiritual growth and personal development.

Therefore, making gratitude a part of your daily routine has positive benefits. Now for those of you who may not be religious or who may even have an aversion to religion, you can still practice gratitude. It is seemingly a transparent phenomenon. You still have the ability to develop an attitude of gratitude by noticing more and more those things—no matter how little they are—that you can be grateful for.

Someone who has just lost their job can still be grateful for the fact that they have their health. In fact losing their job may now give them a new direction in their lives that they wouldn't have found if they had stayed in their job. They may have more time to spend with their family, that they may not have had previously due to the extended time they had to spend at work.

Someone who is ill can still practice gratitude by starting to notice any positive changes—no matter how little they are—that makes them feel better. They can be grateful for the fact that they live in a modern society that provides a well-equipped and highly trained national health service (in-spite of the negative media reporting to the contrary) that can administer modern and cutting-edge medical interventions.

Someone who is depressed can still be grateful for the moments of happiness that they are still able to experience, the supportive family they have, and the fact that they live in a society where we have social support systems that they can call on for help and assistance.

The warm bed we climb into at night, the clean water we have to drink, the roof over our heads, etc., etc., are all things that we can be grateful for.

Developing an attitude of gratitude, combined with Seligman's *Three Blessings* exercise is therefore a powerful and a scientifically proven way to reduce stress, anxiety, worry and depression in our lives and lead us on a path to a happier and more fulfilling lifestyle.

On the next page a 'Count Your Blessings' template is provided for you. All you have to do is do it!!

COUNT YOUR BLESSINGS EXERCISE

List:

   a) Two things that you are grateful for, and
   b) Three things that you feel have affected you in a positive way since getting out of bed this morning.

Day 1	1.	
	2.	
	3.	
	4.	
	5.	
Day 2	1.	
	2.	
	3.	
	4.	
	5.	
Day 3	1.	
	2.	
	3.	
	4.	
	5.	
Day 4	1.	
	2.	
	3.	
	4.	
	5.	

CHAPTER 5.
HOW THOUGHTS BECOME THINGS

So how do our thoughts become things? How does thinking positive actually work? When our brains record an initial experience it is captured by the firing of a particular arrangement of neurons (nerve cells), which leave them lightly connected and primed to fire again, similar to someone walking across an untouched desert and leaving their footprints in the sand. However, for that initial experience to be turned into a more permanent memory the neural network associated to it have to grow, and it does that through the process of *Hebbian association* (Hebb's Law) that we covered earlier on, and this process is also known as *Consolidation*.

FIGURE 1

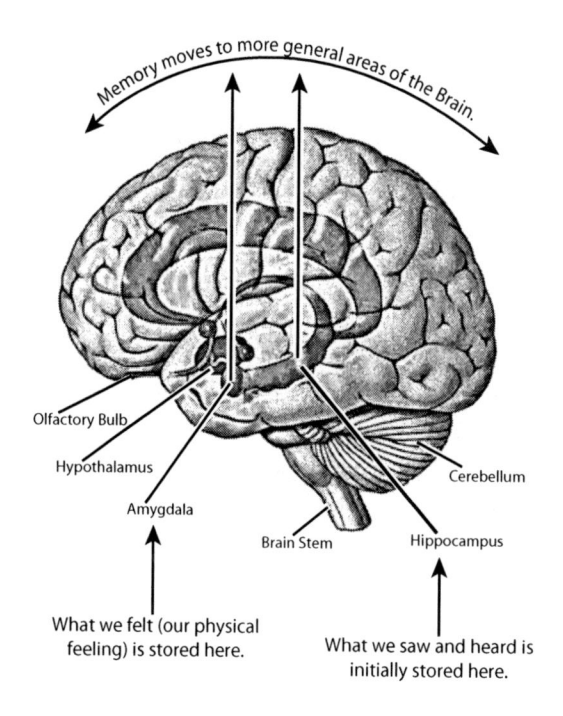

Memory moves to more general areas of the Brain.

Olfactory Bulb
Hypothalamus
Amygdala
Brain Stem
Cerebellum
Hippocampus

What we felt (our physical feeling) is stored here.

What we saw and heard is initially stored here.

During the initial experience (Figure 1) what we see and hear is processed by the hippocampus, and what we feel is processed by the amygdala. What happens next is that the processes of the hippocampus and the amygdala become neurologically associated and that combined memory is then consolidated and moved to more general areas of the brain for storage—a bit like moving something from your computer RAM-drive[9] to your computer hard-drive.

FIGURE 2

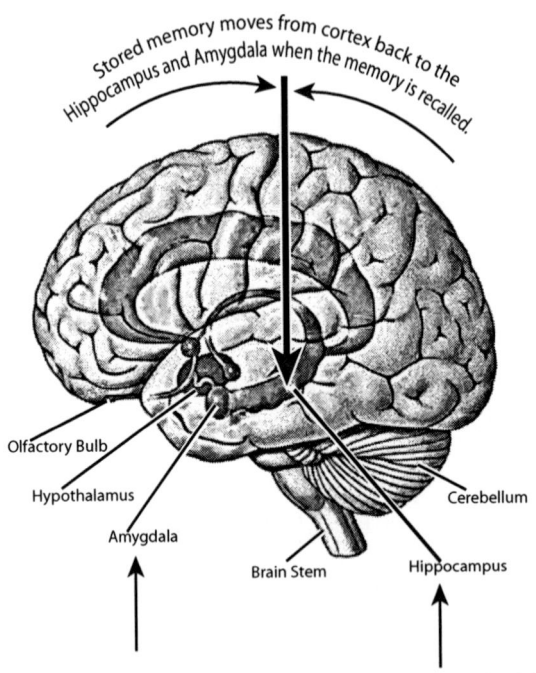

Stored memory moves from cortex back to the Hippocampus and Amygdala when the memory is recalled.

Olfactory Bulb
Hypothalamus
Amygdala
Brain Stem
Cerebellum
Hippocampus

What we initially saw, heard and felt stored becomes 'plastic.'

However, although memory moves from the hippocampus and amygdala to the cortex during consolidation, it is returned to the hippocampus and amygdala for reconsolidation (Figure 2) by the act of memory recall, and this is known as *Reconsolidation*. Using the computer analogy, it is similar to starting up your computer

---

9. RAM stands for 'Random Access Memory' which is basically the working memory of the computer.

FIGURE 3

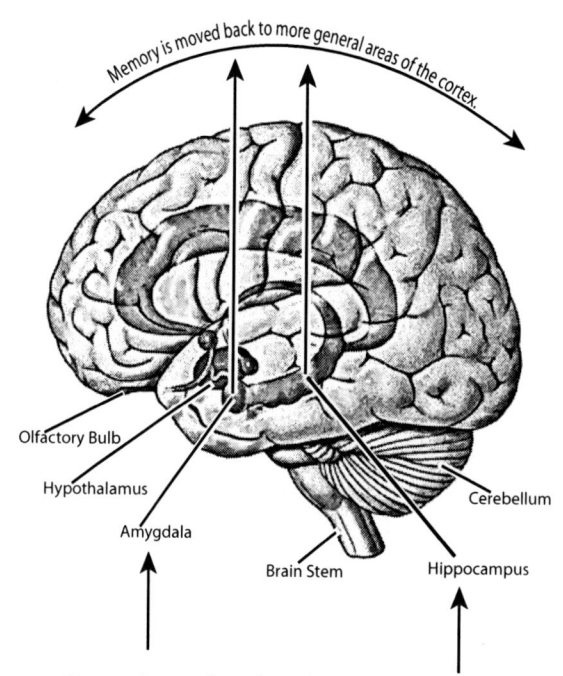

Memory is moved back to more general areas of the cortex

- Olfactory Bulb
- Hypothalamus
- Amygdala
- Brain Stem
- Cerebellum
- Hippocampus

Memory is re-enforced, weakened, transformed

and selecting a specific document on the hard-drive that you had previously created. When the document is opened it is then active and as such is now using the *'Random Access Memory'* [RAM].

When reconsolidation occurs it makes the memory *'plastic'* and vulnerable to change. What this means is that the memory can be updated and re-filed in a different way to when it was initially stored (consolidated) (Figure 3), in much the same way that a document on a computer can be amended, changed and then re-stored back on the computer's hard drive, and if used effectively this can be a powerful and empowering aspect in our personal development. It can be used to strengthen positive beliefs and behaviours, weaken negative beliefs, the meanings associated to certain memories can be re-framed to achieve a more positive outcome, and it can eliminate those out-dated beliefs that hold us back. This is why certain NLP interventions such as changing sub-modality structures, time-line therapy and the 'swish pattern' work.

In the Dalai Lama's book, *The Art of Happiness*[10], he illustrates how this adaptable process of plasticity helps create larger neural networks. The extract is as follows:

> *We are born with brains that are genetically hard wired with certain instinctual behaviour patterns; we are predisposed mentally, emotionally and physically to respond to our environment in ways that enable us to survive. These basic sets of instructions are encoded in countless innate nerve cell activation patterns, specific combinations of brain cells that fire in response to any given event, experience, or thought. But the wiring in our brains is not static, not irrevocably fixed. Our brains are also adaptable. Neuroscientists have documented the fact that the brain can design new patterns, new combinations of nerve cells and neurotransmitters (chemicals that transmit messages between nerve cells) in response to new input. In fact, our brains are malleable, ever changing, reconfiguring their wiring according to new thoughts and experiences. And as a result of learning, the individual neurons themselves change, allowing electrical signals to travel along them more readily. Scientists call the brain's inherent capacity to change 'plasticity.'*

> *This ability to change the brain's wiring, to grow new neural connections, has been demonstrated in experiments such as one conducted by Drs. Avi Karni and Leslie Underleider at the National Institute of Mental Health. In that experiment, the researchers had subjects perform a simple motor task, a finger tapping exercise, and identified the parts of the brain involved in the task by taking an MRI brain scan. The subjects then practiced the finger exercise daily for four weeks, gradually becoming more efficient and quicker at it. At the end of the four-week period, the brain*

---

10. *The Art of Happiness* by HH Dalai Lama & Howard C. Cutler, Mobius (1999), ISBN – 0-340-75015-4.

scan was repeated and showed that the area of the brain involved in the task had expanded; this indicated that the regular practice and repetition of the task had recruited new nerve cells and changed the neural connections that had originally been involved in the task.

This remarkable feature of the brain appears to be the physiological basis for the possibility of transforming our minds. By mobilizing our thoughts and practicing new ways of thinking, we can reshape our nerve cells and change the way our brains work. It is also the basis for the idea that inner transformation begins with learning (new input) and involves the discipline of gradually replacing our 'negative conditioning' (corresponding with our present characteristic nerve cell activation patterns) with 'positive conditioning' (forming new neural circuits). Thus the training of the mind for happiness becomes a very real possibility.

NEGATIVE RECONSOLIDATION STRENGTHENING BAD MEMORIES

Reconsolidation is possibly one reason why some of the recent studies of counseling styles, the type that involve going over past events and talking about the feelings relating to them, tend to deepen an individual's experience of the problem. In essence what this type of counseling is doing is 'reconditioning' a bad event (making the 'groove go deeper'). In other words the negative experience and the negative feelings associated with it become stronger.

However, positive reconsolidation can be very powerful. If we assume that memories are the source of our behaviour, then by changing or updating our thinking associated to those specific memories, or the beliefs and meaning associated with them, we must also change the meaning of every other memory connected to them, resulting in a change in a person's behaviour. This is known as the *'Butterfly Effect.'*

THE BUTTERFLY EFFECT

Professor Edward Lorenz was a mathematician who developed a mathematical model of the way in which air moves around in the atmosphere, for the purpose of predicting weather patters.

One day, towards the end of 1961, Lorenz decided that he wanted to re-examine a run of results he had obtained on his computer. But instead of starting the whole run from the beginning he decided to take a shortcut and start midway through. To re-programme the computer with the initial conditions he typed in the numbers from the earlier printout. As the programme he was using had not been changed the new run should have produced the same printout as the previous one. However, when he compared the new printout with the previous printout he discovered to his amazement that there was no resemblance at all. It was as if he had chosen two random weather patterns out of a hat!

The great difference in Lorenz's printouts arose because the numbers he had entered for the second run were slightly different from the numbers stored in the computer for the first run. In the computer memory six decimal places were entered and stored (0.606832) but on the printout, to save space, just three decimal places appeared (0.606). The difference (one part in a thousand) was, Lorenz assumed, of no consequence, so he re-entered only the three decimal places that had appeared on the initial printout and not the original six decimal places that he had initially entered and stored into the computer.

Because of this initial error a new scientific revolution was launched, and a new science was born. It was called *Chaos Theory*.

Later on, in 1972, Lorenz gave a talk to the American Association for the Advancement of Science entitled *'Predictability: Does the Flap of a Butterfly's Wings in Brazil Set off a Tornado in Texas?'* In the talk he coined the term *'Butterfly Effect'* to describe elegantly how a very small disturbance, such as the movement of a butterfly's wings, in one place can give rise to a series of events that induce enormous consequences in another, far distant, place. Put simply, small deviations in a system can result in large and often unsuspecting results.

Lorenz's theory has had a profound effect in virtually every area of science, bringing about one of the most dramatic changes in mankind's view of nature since the discoveries of Sir Isaac Newton. The small difference he accidentally made, the difference of one part in a thousand, has led to his theory being ranked with Einstein's theory of relativity and quantum mechanics, as the third scientific revolution of the 20th century.

If we consider Lorenz's discovery it is not difficult for us to see why events that we gave meaning to when we were four years old will guide our responses to events when we are ten, which will then guide our responses when we are forty.

Sometimes our lives contain key *'Butterfly'* events, where a small yet insignificant critical moment can have large consequences over time. In terms of our personality they are likely to be the events that trigger a large emotional response. Rapturous applause for a precocious talent in a school play may transform into an Oscar winner twenty years later. Tripping over in front of the same audience may cause a lifetime of performance anxiety and low self-esteem.

However, each individual's response to an event can never be predicted. One child who trips up laughs with the audience, another runs from the stage. It is never the event, but the individual's perception of the event that matters.

For example, if we can go back to the initial Butterfly event (the specific event that has possibly created the larger problem over time), and change or reframe the meaning associated to it, thus discharging the negative association and generating a more positive association, new learning will take place. Once this has occurred it creates a *Butterfly Effect* for all of the other events neurologically associated to that initial significant event that was given that initial negative meaning all those years ago. (This is how interventions such as time-line therapy work).

This is why the conscious attention of learning to focus on positive things regularly, and challenging negative thoughts when they arise, will very possibly bring about dramatic long-term change. As Tony Robbins, the American motivator and guru, says: *"Small changes over time result in large changes in time."* Isn't that so?

If you go down to the gym every day and work out you may not notice day-by-day that you are changing but someone you may bump into who hasn't seen you in years may well comment on how different you look. For those of you who have children you will understand this totally. You see your kids grow up every day so you never necessarily notice the small changes that are happening to them on a consistent basis. But take your child to see a long distant relative that hasn't seen them for years and they are likely to say *"My, haven't you grown!"* The large differences they see was not apparent to us on a day-to-day basis. This is why so many people give up trying too soon when they don't notice any immediate change in the early stages.

We live in a society that expects immediate results, so if we don't get something immediately we tend to dismiss it, wrongly so, as not working. However, if you plant an oak seed in your garden, in good soil and you nurture it and take care of it, eventually it will grow into an oak tree—but that isn't going to happen immediately. It takes time.

If you plant the same seed, however, in poor soil, surrounded by weeds and leave it unchecked and un-nurtured, it is possible that as the initial sprouts starts to break through the soil the weeds will strangle and choke it, hindering it from developing fully.

This is the same with us, including the way we think and what we believe. We need to be aware of our thinking and not allow ourselves to be 'choked' by the tide of negativity that surrounds us. We need to cut out those thoughts from our awareness, to go on a negativity fast if necessary, so that we can learn to train our minds to function differently.

And these little changes, bit by bit, little by little, will lead to massive changes over time. This is why the 'Count Your Blessings' Exercise works.

BACK TO BUDDHISM

Going back to the Dalai Lama's book, *The Art of Happiness*, he presents his approach to working with the mind in pursuit of the path to happiness. In his writing he emphasis that the first step in seeking happiness is learning how negative emotions and behaviour are harmful, and how positive emotions are helpful, not only to us personally but to society and the future of the whole world.

> *In Buddhism, the principle of causality is accepted as a natural law. In dealing with reality, you have to take that law into account. So, for instance, in the case of everyday experiences, if there are certain types of events that you do not desire, then the best method of ensuring that the event does not take place is to make sure that the causal conditions that normally give rise to that event no longer arise. Similarly, if you want a particular event or experience to occur, then the logical thing to do is to seek and accumulate the causes and conditions that give rise to it.*

It is interesting to note that we are now only just beginning to accept in the West what Buddhism has been teaching and practicing in the east for over twenty-five hundred years. It must make sense to accept that the mind and body are one inseparable entity. One affects the other, and therefore they are intrinsically linked and entwined. Each thought we have permeates every aspect of our mind and body, right down to our basic bio-cellular structure, and even further into our atomic and sub-atomic building blocks. What we focus on we draw into our lives. Our thoughts are like magnets that attract more of the same into being, so we all need to be asking ourselves one fundamental question: what do we want to attract into our lives?

Think about it. The brain cannot process a negative command, and what I mean is that if we focus our energy and effort on what we don't want—then we bring the very thing we don't want into conscious attention. Then the principle of causality helps *to* create the reality of the manifestation of the very thing we don't desire.

We need to spend more time on constructive thought processes, and on learning how to focus on what we do want.

Here's one tip that you can apply straight away. In many meetings, 80% of the time can be devoted to understanding why a problem occurred with only 20% of the time allocated to the solution. Why not devote 80% of the time to the solution and 20% of the time to the problem? In this way a meeting could be far more constructive in bringing more positive solutions. If not, then we will continue to waste our time discussing why things won't work, and in turn continue to prove these perceptions right.

Do one small thing each day that benefits you. If you do this you will not achieve three hundred and sixty-five new things a year from now. You will achieve much, much more. And this is because of the law of compound interest. If you put a pound in a savings account every day for a year you will accrue interest on your savings in addition to what you invest, and positive and creative thinking works in the same way.

That is what the Law of Attraction is all about.

Chapter 6.
The Law of Attraction and Interaction

If you have you ever stood on a railway platform when a fast train roars through, you will know something about the Law of Attraction and Interaction. As the train arrives it pushes an air pressure wave forwards and outwards which blows your hat off. Also, as it passes it tends to suck you in towards it. This is why you are advised to stand back, away from the platform edge.

The same thing happens with boats. Ever notice how smaller boats tend to move closer to the larger ones when in the sea? This is because attraction and interaction affects boats. Each boat will make it's own pressure waves and suction zones. When the boats pass close together there comes a point when both suction zones are adjacent and the boats are dragged even closer together, sometimes with alarming force.

Funnily enough, the same thing happens with our thoughts. Have you ever worried about something and noticed how more worried thoughts come into mind? Have you ever looked forward to something and noticed how many more pleasurable thoughts come into mind?

The fact is once you start focussing on something, that thought attracts other similar thoughts. Why? Because neurons that fire together, wire together. The more we think a certain way the more we will attract more similar thoughts into our conscious awareness.

This is called 'the Law of Attraction' and it is one of the greatest unseen forces in the universe. Just as we have the law of gravity, which is an unseen phenomenon, the Law of Attraction is also a phenomenon, which many of the great thinkers have known about for centuries, and which is included in every major religion's philosophy.

> *Everything that is coming into your life you are attracting into your life. And it's attracted to you by virtue of the images you're holding in your mind. It's what you're thinking. Whatever is going on in your mind, you are attracting to you.*
>
> Quote from the DVD
What the Bleep do we know?[11]

The Law of Attraction states that like attracts like, so when you think a certain thought you are attracting other similar thoughts to you.

GOOD VIBRATIONS

Ever had a 'good feeling' about something? That is simply the result of having good thoughts. Ever felt 'bad'? Hey, guess what, that's the result of having bad thoughts. Change the way you think and you change the way you feel.

But how do our thoughts actually affect our being? Well all things vibrate and all human beings vibrate at certain frequencies. At the smallest sub-atomic scale, sub-atomic particles resonate at a set frequency. Changing this frequency not only changes the structure of the sub-atomic particle but also it's relationship with other particles. Over time, a continual frequency can result in continual changes at the atomic, cellular and organic levels.

For example, if you tuned in to your favourite radio station everyday, say on a frequency of 88.2Hz (Hertz = frequency of 88.2 cycles per second) you would only hear the music played by that station and not music played on another station transmitting on a different frequency. If the music you listen to regularly on the radio station you are tuned into cheers you up then the music is affecting you emotionally in a positive way. If however, you tuned into a radio station that was playing music or discussing information that you didn't like or that upset you, then music or discussion is affecting you emotionally in a negative way. A simple switching

---

11. DVD :*What the Bleep do we know!?*—www.whatthebleep.com

of channels would provide you with a different stimulus, and the same is true of our thoughts.

In essence we are like human transmission towers that emit certain frequencies. Just as the BBC, ITV, Channel 4, and all the Sky channels transmit their programmes on different frequencies, we transmit our thoughts in the same way. So, just as you choose what channel to watch, you can do the same with your thoughts—if you don't like what you're thinking about, you can always change channels. You can focus your mind on what you want to focus on. The alternative is that you let others decide what you focus on and choose what you think about.

All thoughts are energy (vibrations) that create frequencies at the sub-atomic level. If we tune into the right way of thinking we produce the right frequencies. Over time this will create the right kind of changes further up the chain at the atomic, cellular and organic levels.

In short, your thoughts over time have created the person you are now, and your thoughts from now on will create the person that you will become in the future, as they are what make you focus in a certain direction. It is estimated that the average human being has between 45,000 to 60,000 thoughts a day and the more we use our dominant thoughts, the more that way of thinking will become second nature and the more it will provide a stimulating environment in which our cells will thrive.

Therefore, the first step in changing our lives for the better is to become aware of what we think about, and *how* what we think about is effecting or lives. We must choose to think about those things that we want to think about and *not think* about those things that we don't want.

As Richard Bandler, one of the founders of NLP, says:

"If you don't run your own brain for your own benefit others will gladly run it for you for their benefit."

The powerful thing to understand is that your current thoughts are creating your future life. What you think about the most, or focus on the most, will appear as your life.

How many of us are simply re-living yesterday every day?

However, there is a shortcut to changing the way you think! It is impossible to feel bad and at the same time have good thoughts. Therefore, by simply training our brain to focus on more good thinking than bad thinking, we can begin to change how we feel more permanently. Furthermore, reframing situations to find the positive in every situation can change your feelings in an instant!

The simple fact is that each of us has the ability to make better choices in our lives by applying our thoughts in a more positive, constructive and functional way. This allows us to enable ourselves to take more direct control over the way we think, thus permitting us to better manage occupational and personal change. This also lets us reduce our personal stress levels, through a better understanding of how our own thoughts and actions effect our behaviour and well-being.

> *I never hit a shot even in practice without having a sharp in-focus picture of it in my head. It's like a colour movie. First, I "see" the ball where I want it to finish, nice and white and sitting up high on the bright green grass. Then the scene quickly changes, and I "see" the ball going there: its path, trajectory, and shape, even its behaviour on landing. Then there's a sort of fade-out, and the next scene shows me making the kind of swing that will turn the previous images into reality. Only at the end of this short private Hollywood spectacular do I select a club and step up to the ball.*
>
> Jack Nicklaus

THE LAW OF REVERSED EFFECT— WHAT YOU RESIST PERSISTS

The 'Law of Reversed Effect,' or 'what you resist, persists,' is also based on the Law of Attraction.

If you really don't want something don't think about it too much or you are likely to create it through the process of resisting it. This is because what we resist we give energy to. Remember too that the mind cannot focus on a negative command, so as we discussed earlier 'Don't drop that' becomes 'Drop that—don't' and the child ends up dropping the drink. This is the law of reversed effect in action. What you are attempting to prevent or resist, occurs.

If our mind therefore, is dominated by thoughts of things that we would like to get rid of, like an illness or a disease, or if we are in a relationship in which we have become dominated by all that is wrong with it, we can end up making ourselves ill or making the relationship worse by the constant focus of attention in that area. If a particular person makes you angry and you end up continually wishing that you could avoid that person, you may find that your paths cross more often. If someone is constantly worrying about lack of money because they are trying to resist losing money, they end up giving energy to those thought processes and as a result will possibly end up losing more money. This is because what we are trying to resist—persists, by the simple fact that we give energy to that which we try or want to avoid happening.

Ask yourself this question: Would you fight harder to stop someone stealing two-thousand pounds from you, or to generate two-thousand pounds in additional income?

Someone I know for example was cheated out of two-thousand pounds by a business partner. He was so incensed with being 'ripped-off' that his mind became dominated with getting his money back. To this extent he spent every moment of every day consumed with the negative thoughts associated with being cheated out of his money. He followed the person who owed him money, sitting outside of his offices and his house. He hired lawyers and took the man to court. In the end, he ended up spending over twenty thousand pounds in costs trying to get back the two-thousand pounds that he was cheated out of.

He was so busy trying to prove a point that he lost focus of what really mattered. As such he fell victim to the law of reversed effect.

What the Law of Reversed Effect demonstrates is that what we fight against we give energy to, and by doing so, we create it's existence and so experience it more.

'Energy Flows Where Attention Goes'

For example, if we constantly think of ourselves as being 'victims,' we will adopt a 'victim mentality,' and we will start seeing ourselves as being 'victims of circumstance.' If we constantly think of ourselves as being poor, for example, then what we fear is poverty, and because the Law of Attraction and the Law of Reversed Effect are basically two sides of the same coin, we end up attracting those circumstances and situations into our lives that justify our lack of money. Such negative prophecies therefore, become self-fulfilling ones.

It is at times like these when our faith will be tested. Our ability to decide what we focus on cannot be determined by what happens externally. It has to be determined by what happens internally. And as all things begin with a thought process we have to be mindful of our thinking and not become emotionally influenced or hijacked.

The Fellowship of the Miserables

I was at a seminar a while ago listening to a speaker who came up with a great line that epitomised some of the negative people that he (and I) come across every now and then. He was explaining that when he first started his business he would go down to his local pub for a beer and to meet up with his mates whom he had known for some time. What he found odd was that his friends who had known him for many years, the same friends who he had worked with for a long time, and the same friends whose families went out together, and who supported each other through good times and bad, were now seemingly 'willing him to fail.'

When asked by others: "*How is the business going,*" he would reply, "*Great. It's brilliant being my own boss.*" But to his surprise, he would find that instead of supporting his feelings, they would reply as if to warn him of impending doom, with comments such as: "*Well things may be OK now, but loads of people who go self-employed go bankrupt,*" or "*I know someone who used to do what your doing, and they went bust and lost everything, house, car—oh, and their marriage failed.*"

At first this really got him down. It made him doubt his own ability and his own instinct. This is a guy who had worked out the risk. He had calculated the odds carefully before going self-employed. His wife was supporting him and he was driven by a desire to improve the quality of life for himself and his family—so why are his friends filling his head full of negative thoughts? Why aren't they encouraging him? Why are they 'dragging him down?' One very basic reason is fear—which is driven by the law of reversed effect.

When someone is bold enough to step outside the box, to step up to the mark and be counted, to place conformity and complacency behind him or her, some others actually fear that they will be successful. And the reason isn't too hard to decipher. If one person can do it then the possibility is that others can do it too. But hang on a minute, this means that if that one person is successful, and we could also do that, but choose not to—then isn't it better if they fail? Then at least we can say *"we told you so"* which self-justifies our not needing to attempt something as equally bold, which in turn self-justifies our need to conform and to feed our ever-increasing sense of complacency, wrapped up in phrases like: *"Well it could be worse,"* or *"At least things aren't as bad as . . ."* and so on.

Well this guy had a phrase for these types or groups of people. He called them *"The Fellowship of the Miserables"* and I think he was bang on the money with that description.

Have you met a member of the 'The Fellowship Of The Miserables?' I bet you have. Have you nearly become one? Be careful, if you have, cancel your membership immediately! I can now see them coming a mile off. They thrive on someone else's misfortune and gorge on another person's mishaps, primarily because it serves them to see someone else fail as it justifies the fact that they shouldn't do anything.

Now this is not a brotherhood or fellowship that any forward thinking person should ever consider joining. When I am confronted with one or a few of these draining, energy-sucking leeches, I either kindly excuse myself and go and talk to someone else, or, if I really feel like playing with them, I'll pour salt on them (leeches hate salt) by stating something like *"Well I'm glad that didn't happen to me, otherwise I wouldn't have all this money and free-time to have all the fun I'm having,"* and what is interesting is that their response to that is normally: *"Well that's because your lucky."* Lucky!? The harder I work the luckier I seem to get.

Just Do It!

Here's the reality. If your not getting out of life what you want, it is because you are not doing what you should be doing to achieve it. Now I know that what I have just said is possibly a bit blunt and it may upset you, and I apologise if it did. But unfortunately it is true. How many people dream of improving their quality of life by getting a better job, working for themselves, earning more money, etc., yet do nothing to achieve it except sit and wait for luck to pass by and knock on their door? Let me give you an example. I have someone who is a good friend of mine, who I have known for many years who has recently started his own business.

When he was looking to start his own business he had done his homework well. He had figured out what he needed to earn and how he would go about getting it. He had a very comprehensive business and marketing plan and he had worked out where he would market his business to get the best possible return and response rate to his marketing strategy.

One evening while we were having a drink and catching up with each other he said to me: *"The business isn't doing too well at the moment. I'm struggling to get work, and if I don't find some work soon I may have to consider closing the business and going back to being employed."*

This shocked me a little as the level headed and inspired man I knew a few months back was now talking like a depressive. *"Why is that?"* I asked him.

"Well," he said, *"I just can't seem to get any business. No one seems to want any training and I haven't got anything lined up for the next month, so things are looking dire. It has to be the current market at the moment, everyone's struggling and I know I'm a good trainer. Maybe the current financial situation in the UK is having a knock on effect into people buying in training, and I can't see things picking up. In short, I guess that it's just the wrong time to be in this kind of business."*

"How many letters have you sent out today?" I asked.
"Today?" he said, sounding a bit surprised.
"Yes, today!" I replied once more.
"Well, none," he said.

"Ok, how many mail-shots have you done this week?" I asked.

"Eh? None," was his reply.

"OK, how many letters have you sent out this month?" I asked.

"Well, maybe about ten to twenty," was his reply.

"OK, how many phone calls have you made today, this week, this month, to prospective clients or potential leads?" I asked.

"Eh? None really. I did follow up a call we had from someone who was referred to us, but I didn't want to call him again in case he thought I was being 'pushy'."

"The reason you're not getting any business isn't because of the current market," I said. "The reason you're not getting any business is because you're not doing what you need to do to get it."

Now this is a fact of life. You can have the best product in the world but if no one knows you have it then your marketing strategy is similar to winking in the dark. In other words, you know what you doing but no one else does.

If you want something to happen you have to create the happening. You have to get out there and let people or businesses know what you've got and why they should use you. If you think you will be successful and take one action a day to lead you towards your goal you will attract other positive situations, opportunities and circumstances into your conscious awareness to make that perception a reality.

However, if you believe that you will fail or are destined to be unsuccessful, you are likely not to take the necessary actions, or possibly not even be able to think of what actions to take that could prove that perception wrong. As a result you will only notice those situations, events and circumstances that are self-serving and will self-justify your perception of failure.

Fact: There is no point walking forward while always looking back.

So, if I just Think About Being Rich Will I Become Rich?

In the film Evan Almighty, Evan's wife Joan, prays for the family to become closer. What happens in the film is that God, in the form of Morgan Freeman, appears to Evan and commands him to build an Ark. Other strange things also start to happen to Evan. He begins to grow a beard and long hair, and no matter how quickly he shaves the beard grows back immediately. He is also given a robe similar to what Noah would have worn, and no matter whether he takes it off of covers it up, he always ends up dressed in this ancient garment. As a result Evan's wife begins to think he is having some form of breakdown and eventually decides to leave him, and goes away with her three children to her mothers. While sitting in a café thinking, Evan's wife Joan is unknowingly approached by God (played by Morgan Freeman) in the form of a waiter, who strikes up a conversation with her. As a result she explains her predicament to him and in return God tells her that the story of Noah isn't just about the great flood. He tells her that it is a story of partnership and togetherness. He explains that in the Bible Noah built the Ark with his family and the animals came in pairs, a sign of togetherness. In explaining this he says the following to her:

> *Let me ask you something, if someone prays for patience do you think God gives them patience or does he give them the opportunity to be patient? If they pray for courage does God give them courage or the opportunity to be courageous? If someone prays for family to be closer, do you think God zaps them with warm, fuzzy feelings, or does he give them opportunity to love each other?*

This is how the Law of Attraction works. It is not going to make you wealthier, healthier, or happier, but it is going to present you with an abundance of opportunities to become wealthier, healthier and happier. By tuning ourselves into the right frequency we will attract to us those situations, opportunities and events that will provide us with the opportunities. All we have to do is notice them and act upon them. But to do that we have to be looking in the right direction to notice them, we have to be focusing on the positive, not the negative. Otherwise we will not notice what we aren't looking for.

"Luck is when preparation meets opportunity."

For example, as I was writing this chapter I was looking for something to illustrate the Law of Attraction in action. As a family we all sit down around 9pm to unwind and watch a movie, have a glass of wine and generally relax. I had selected a movie on Sky Box Office, the movies that you have to pay for to watch. It was *Dan in Real Life* starring Steve Carell. We all sat down at the start and then all of a sudden we lost the sky signal, but it was only on that channel and a couple of others. I checked the signal strength on the skybox and that was fine and the vast majority of all of the other channels worked as normal. In an attempt to get it back I played with the skybox, unplugged it and re-set it, and I even got up a ladder to fiddle about with the satellite dish, but to no avail. I just couldn't get the channel to work for the movie I wanted to watch. So in frustration I started looking at what was on the other channels and we came across the movie *Evan Almighty*. Now we had seen it before but my wife said that she enjoyed it and wouldn't mind seeing it again so we opted to watch it once more. What was interesting was as I watched it I found the above example that I could use from the movie to illustrate the Law of Attraction. So is that luck or was the opportunity being presented to me in the hope that I would notice it? I tend to believe the latter as it happens to me now all too often. For example, as you read this book you will notice that I reference lots of other books. As I began writing this book I would get the urge to go to the bookshelf in my office and pick up a particular book. I have also at times walked into a bookshop, or been browsing Amazon, when a book or an audio has caught my eye. Sometimes I see the same book or audio more than once. If this happens I take it as an opportunity being presented and I usually buy it. In the vast majority of cases what I have acquired has been of benefit to me, and the more I do it, the better I get at noticing those things that provide me with opportunity. In doing so I have found inspiration and factual evidence that I have not only used in the writing of this book, but opportunities to take action that have a positive effect in my business, my family and my health.

So if you want to be rich focus on having wealth, not lack of money and you will soon begin to notice the circumstances and events that will come your way that will provide you with the opportunities to become wealthier. If you want better health, focus on being healthier, notice more and more each day only on the positive aspects of your well-being, how much health you have and then circumstances and events will present themselves to you that will allow you to take action to become healthier. If you want a more loving relationship with the person you are with then start by noticing all of the positive things that are good in that relationship and very soon events and circumstances will reveal themselves to you that will give you the opportunity to demonstrate your love.

"When the student is ready the Master will appear."

Consider Paul Potts, the opera singer who won the *Britain's Got Talent* talent show. Prior to the show Paul suffered terribly with a lack of confidence. Prior to becoming famous Paul was employed as a mobile phone salesman. However, he always wanted to have a career as a signer, and his dream, in his words *"was to do what he was born to do"*—sing! He had the belief in himself that he was a good singer, but it was his constant struggle with his confidence that was stopping him pursuing his dream. However the *Britain's Got Talent* talent show provided him with the opportunity to be confident and demonstrate his belief. And the rest, as they say, is history. Paul had obviously practiced for many years to become such a talented signer and the *Britain's Got Talent* talent show was the circumstance that arrived in his life when he was ready for the opportunity to be presented.

Does this mean that we always get what we want first time? No. Does this mean that we will always get it right first time? No. However, each attempt is an opportunity for us to discover something new, possibly something that we wouldn't have ever come across had we not made that initial attempt at something.

'Doing the same thing the same way and expecting a different result'.

Definition of Insanity

As Tony Robbins[12], the great American motivational speaker, self-help guru and developer of the best selling *Personal Power* audio programmes, says: *"If you do something and it doesn't work, do something else. If you do something else and that doesn't work, do something else. Keep doing something else until you find something that works."*

---

12. View Tony Robbins' website at: www.tonyrobbins.com.

CHAPTER 7.
FALL SEVEN TIMES—
STAND UP EIGHT
(JAPANESE PROVERB)

Do you know the percentage of the time an aircraft is off course when flying to its pre-determined destination? Well it might surprise you to know that it is off-course approximately 95% of the time!

As soon as the aircraft takes off it is affected by wind-speed and various other conditions that take it off-course. However, because the aircrew continually monitors the aircraft's progress and flight-path through use of the aircraft's navigational instruments, the aircraft is continually brought back on track so that it can arrive at the right destination at the right time.

The human race is so good at being able to use feedback to monitor and correct, that we can even send a spacecraft millions of miles away into a far flung part of the universe, and have it arrive at it's planetary destination to within a few seconds of its expected time of arrival, even if no such craft had even been sent to that planet before! Yet when it comes down to what we want to achieve personally, we find ourselves incapable of duplicating models used by thousands of people who have already achieved those goals, and in doing so left us with a clear map with explicit directions and instructions of how they did it. In great contrast to this, many find reasons why they couldn't duplicate what has already been achieved. Maybe fear of success scares them? Maybe it is a belief that they were not meant to be successful, that success is the privilege of other 'luckier' people.

Also, some people may give up too easily. If they try something once and it doesn't work, that is all the proof they need not to try something different, or do things in a different way. However, if we were to take these chances, if we were willing to try different options or approaches—we would possibly open up new ways of thinking that could only serve to benefit us. Sometimes what we are hoping to achieve is just below the surface of our conscious awareness, striving to break through. Yet we give up, so the seed isn't watered and fed and eventually resigns itself to a life below the surface.

Think about an athlete. The 2008 Olympics has just begun as I started writing this book. As I watch the various sportsmen and women compete, I am reminded of the years and years of continual effort that they must have put in to their training and the sacrifices that they made in order to get them into their respective Olympic squads. These athletes meet failure everyday, but they do not view it as failure. If they did they would lose their motivation and drive to win. They see each attempt as something they can review and improve on, taking them ever closer to their goal of being the best they can be.

I read some research which stated that the average sports-person fails over 75% of the time, but their ability to keep going, and their focus on continual improvement is what finally makes them the best at what they do. Imagine the amount of pain, suffering, toil and sweat that goes into a modern athlete's training regime to prepare them for the Olympics. Imagine four years of intense constant training, special diets, time away from their families, and many of these great sports-people do it whilst juggling their jobs and family life also. What makes the great athlete greater than the rest is their ability to focus on the long-term goal. Their ability to visualize what all the hard work will accomplish. They also learn to love what they do, and the reason is simple—if you really, really enjoy something you don't need discipline.

> "I hated every minute of training, but I said, don't quit. Suffer now and live the rest of your life as a champion."
> Muhammad Ali

THOMAS EDISON

Here is something to consider. Think about Thomas Edison, who is famous for inventing the light bulb. Edison actually made over ten thousand attempts before finally producing a light bulb that worked. After about seven thousand attempts, Edison was asked why he kept trying when he had obviously failed thousands of times. Undeterred and completely focused on his goal, Edison responded by stating that he hadn't failed, he had simply found seven thousand ways *not* to invent the light bulb! Could you imagine how things could be if Edison had decided not to continue trying? One man changed the way we live with that sole focus.

ERNEST SHAKLETON

Another one of my heroes is Ernest Shakleton, who was once quoted as saying: *"Once the last mark has been reached or has passed, set yourself another."* His ability to change a failed attempt to reach the South Pole has become one of the greatest feats of survival and leadership ever, and is true testimony to the human race's ability to overcome adversity and achieve success.

Ernest Shakleton was an explorer whose expedition to the South Pole in 1915 ended in disaster when his ship, the Endurance, became trapped in the ice, eventually sinking ten months later. As a result, his goal of reaching the South Pole ended. So instead, he set himself a new goal—that of getting himself and his 27 men home safely.

He managed to get his crew into three 23-foot (8m) small boats and sailed them to Elephant Island, where they could live in relative safety. He then took one of these small boats with five of his crew to find help. In the winter of 1916, these six men spent sixteen days crossing eight hundred miles of some of the most dangerous oceans in the world, to eventually reach South Georgia. However, their test of endurance wasn't over yet.

On reaching South Georgia, the six men landed on an uninhabited part of the island. They then had to cross 26 miles of mountains, glaciers and snowfields, considered impassable at the time, to reach the whaling station on the other side. Shakleton then somehow managed to secure himself another ship and sailed the eight hundred miles back to Elephant Island where he rescued his men.

In short, when Shakleton's goal of reaching the South Pole ended he set himself a new goal—that of getting all of his crew back home alive. As a result not one of his men died and his exploits went down in history as one of the greatest feats of leadership ever.

Despite our best efforts to design a life that focuses only on what we want, life will still throw challenges our way. These challenges, in relation to the aircraft analogy, may temporarily take us off course.

Consider sailing. Many sailors who navigate sailing boats deal with this every time they set out to sea. They will encounter wind conditions that they have no direct control over, so what they do is learn to use the wind to their advantage, as opposed to fighting it. They do this by changing the positioning of the sails, called 'tacking,' and by using the rudder to enable to wind to be used—whichever direction it is coming from, to get the boat to where they want it to go. These sailors don't just let the wind blow them to places they don't want to go; instead they continually tack and turn so that they use the wind to their advantage—so they get exactly to their intended destinations.

This is a good way to view life. Life will continue to throw things our way that we didn't expect so the real secret is not what happens, but how we deal with what happens and our attitude towards how we deal with what happens.

One great example of man's attitude towards life can be found in the story of Viktor Frankl.

VIKTOR FRANKL

"Everything can be taken from a man but the last of the human freedoms—to choose one's attitude in any given set of circumstances, to choose one's own way."
Viktor E. Frankl

Viktor Frankl was a doctor of psychiatry when he found himself involved in the Nazi occupation of his homeland. His father, mother, brother and wife died in the bestial and brutal conditions of the camps or were gassed to death. With the exception of his sister, his entire family died or were executed in the Nazi concentration camps.

With every possession and loved one taken from him, and with the constant everyday struggle against hunger, malnutrition, cold and the uncertainty of death ever present, Frankl's survival and observation of life in the camps make for fantastic reading.

At times he lived with up to fifteen hundred other captives in a shed that was built to hold no more than two hundred. There was not enough room to lie down or squat on the bare, cold ground and a five-ounce piece of bread was the only food they might have to eat in a four-day period.

As a result of the endless drudgery, bitterness, cold, hunger, the primitive and inhumane conditions, the constant danger of death and the sense of hopelessness of their situation, the thought of suicide was always present in the minds of many.

Those that survived this situation, had to adopt certain ways of thinking and behaving. One of the stories that Frankl recounts is about of one of his friends who had arrived at Auschwitz several weeks before him. He had managed to sneak himself into Frankl's hut to pass on some tips on how to survive. His advice, as recounted in Frankl's book, *Man's Search for Meaning*[13], is as follows:

> *But one thing I beg of you . . . shave daily, if at all possible, even if you have to use a piece of glass to do it . . . even if you have to give your last piece of bread for it. You will look younger and the scraping will make your cheeks look ruddier. If you want to stay alive, there is only one way: look fit for work. If you even limp, because, let us say, you have a small blister on your heel, and an SS man spots this, he will wave you aside and the next day you are sure to be gassed. Do you know what we mean by a 'Moslem?' A man who looks miserable, down and out, sick and emaciated, and who cannot manage hard physical labor any longe . . . that is a 'Moslem.' Sooner or later, usually sooner, every 'Moslem' goes to the gas chambers. Therefore, remember:*

---

13. *Man's Search for Meaning* by Viktor E. Frankl, Rider & Co (2004), ISBN: 9781844132393.

shave, stand and walk smartly; then you need not be afraid of gas.

What this extract from Frankl's book illustrates is the need to look *"fit for work."* Even if you do not feel fit—you should look it. Now this is absolutely first class advice. If you look good, you will end up feeling good. This is known as the 'physiological/psychological' loop. Haven't you ever got dressed up to go out and *"felt like a million dollars?"* Have you ever had to go down to the gym when you felt tired, but felt energized and revitalized when you returned? Have you ever had to make an impression and to do so adopted a more positive posture or pose, spoken with authority or walked with purpose?

A basic fact is that if we change the way we look and act then we change the way we think. Think about the opposite. Ever seen or spoken to someone who is depressed? Well if you have, you will have noticed how they sit, stand and walk. It is as if the world is on their shoulders. They speak with an air of despair and apathy. However, if they changed the way they looked and acted, they would change the way they felt.

In the concentration camps Frankl soon discovered that it was their attitude towards the situation they found themselves in, not the situation itself that determined how they coped.

Frankl realized that it was not what happened to him that was important. He had no control over any aspect of his environment and was aware of the fact that the Nazi's could do whatever they wanted with his emaciated body. They could not, however, control his inner identity, nor could they control how he could choose to respond in any given set of circumstances. He controlled his inner self. He saw that there was a gap between what happened to him and his reaction, and in that gap he had the power and freedom to choose his response. In short, Frankl refused to accept that his situation was hopeless. He maintained his ability to make decisions and choices. He didn't resign himself to the apathy of 'learned helplessness.' This is what Frankl refers to as *"the last of the human freedoms."* Frankl became aware of the fact that his own choices, not his circumstances, defined his identity. No matter how bare or brutal his environment, he was in control of how he would choose to respond. If he could do that, so can each and every one of us.

> *"Life is ten per-cent what happens and ninety per-cent how we respond to it."*
>
> Charles Swindoll

JIM LOVELL

Jim Lovell was the Commander of the ill-fated Apollo 13 space mission. He managed to get his crew home safely after damage to their spacecraft not only brought to an end their dreams of landing on the moon, but nearly resulted in his death and that of his two fellow crew members. At the time the fate of the Apollo mission was being screened on television, a television news reporter showed an interview that he had done with Jim Lovell before they left for the moon. In the interview, the reporter asked Lovell if he was ever scared.

In response, Lovell recalled a time when he was on exercise on a clear, but dark night over the Sea of Japan. He was flying in a Banshee jet aircraft during a combat exercise and was trying to get back to his aircraft carrier. However, his radar had jammed so he couldn't locate his ship and his homing signal (the signal that would tell him which direction to fly in to get back) was jammed because someone was using the same frequency on the mainland of Japan. He even lost his navigational instruments and lights in the aircraft cockpit due to an electrical problem, so he wasn't able to locate his exact position. Lovell didn't know whether he was heading in the right or the wrong direction, and he was also low on fuel. It was then that he said the following:

> *I know I'm running out of fuel so I'm thinking about ditching in the ocean and I look down there and then in the darkness there's this green trail, it's like a long carpet that's just laid out right beneath me and it was the algae, right. It was that phosphorescent stuff that gets churned*

up in the wake of a big ship and it was just leading me home. If my cockpit lights hadn't shorted out there's no way I'd have ever been able to see that, so you never know what events are going to transpire to get you home. [14]

Lovell's response reflects his belief that even when everything seems to be against you, there will always be something that you would not have noticed had it not have been for the circumstances that you found yourself in.

One common trait shared by all of these great people in this chapter is belief. They had absolute, unwavering belief in their ability to bring about the outcomes they desired. Edison had the belief that he would invent the electric light-bulb, Shakleton believed he would bring all of his men home alive, and his men believed in him, Viktor Frankl believed he would survive and that his life had purpose and Jim Lovell believed fully that a solution would be found to their predicament and that he would survive the Apollo 13 mission. Their beliefs are what kept them going. Their unwavering trust in what they had set their minds to achieve made what they achieved possible, even in the face of what would seem like insurmountable obstacles to many. This proves you should never give up!

---

14. DVD: *Apollo 13*, Starring Tom Hanks as Jim Lovell.

CHAPTER 8.
BELIEFS

"It's lack of faith that makes people afraid of meeting challenges, and I believed in myself."
                                        Muhammad Ali

What we believe has a far greater influence on our life than any objective truth will ever have. Our beliefs are windows through which we view our perceptions of the world we inhabit.

Our beliefs determine our focus, what we pay attention to, which ultimately determines the direction we take in life, and the view we have of life in general. For example, if you believe that you have *'no control'* in your life, or if you believe that *'all men/women are bad,'* or *'the job gets you down,'* then sadly, you will focus your thoughts in those directions and attract those things into your life, thus providing the evidence you require to satisfy what you believe. In essence, what we choose to believe will determine the focus of our conscious awareness, which in turn, will determine the decisions we make. These decisions will inevitably affect the direction our life takes and the outcomes it produces.

Our beliefs are very important to the quality of our lives. Yet so many of us are too quick, and readily willing to adopt certain beliefs, and accept some things as being true—without questioning them. This is how many of the world's religious, social, political, cultural and business communities develop and promote the wide range of dogma that we passively accept and let decide for us WHO we are and HOW we should live our lives.

And believe me, families are no exception to the development and promotion of dogmatic beliefs. I know many people who have struggled to be happy simply because they have been consistently told things like: *"depression runs in the family"* or *"your just like your mother/father, they were always unlucky in love."* These or similar limiting statements end up being etched so deeply in one's mental grooves that they become the very reality that some people experience on a daily basis. In essence, they end up believing the personal dogma imposed upon them by outside influences.

However, beliefs are not necessarily true. They are, in fact, only what we believe to be true. For example, for many thousands of years people believed the world to be flat, and that if they went too far they would fall off the edge. This 'limiting belief' restricted many people who would never go "further than the eye could see" for fear they would fall off the earth. It was also generally believed that the world was the centre of the universe and that the sun and the planets revolved around the earth.

We all know now that is not true thanks to Nicolaus Copernicus and his treatise, *De revolutionibus orbium coelestium* (*On the Revolutions of the Celestial Spheres*), published in 1543. His work is regarded as the origin point of modern astronomy and the defining realisation that helped fuel the Scientific Revolution. The fact that those old limiting beliefs no longer exist now is mainly due to the brave exploits of those great thinkers, explorers and scientists who challenged those restrictive and limiting world views of their time, and then went on to prove them wrong. However, just think for a moment how things would be different for us now if those great people had just accepted the mainstream beliefs of their times and decided not to take the risks they did. How would the world that we have come to know now be different if they hadn't had the courage to challenge the dogma and beliefs that existed back then?

You see, sometimes all it takes is just one counter-example or one new idea to disprove a long-established and widely-held belief, which, by doing so, can transform not only a person, but sometimes an entire world-view of things.

One such example is that of Roger Bannister, who on the 6th May 1954, did what everyone else believed was impossible—he ran a mile in under four minutes. For years, the 4-minute mile was considered not merely unreachable, but also, according to some physiologists and other academically-qualified professionals, dangerous to the health of any athlete who attempted to reach it. They confidently stated that running a mile in under four minutes could result in all sorts of damage to the human body and our internal bodily organs and systems.

However, the amazing fact was that within one year of Roger Bannister breaking the 4-minute mile, another three hundred runners did just the same thing. In essence, it only took one counter-example for everyone else to change a limiting belief—even one promoted by so called 'professionals.'

SELF-BELIEF AND PERFORMANCE

In one of the most detailed studies ever conducted into the effects of self-belief on performance, psychologist Albert Bandura (the originator of social cognitive theory) discovered that a person's genuine beliefs about their capabilities can be a more accurate predictor of their future levels of performance than any actual results they had produced in the past. In other words, the way you think about yourself in relation to the challenges you are currently facing in your life will have a profound effect on your ability to succeed.

This is a very important fact to consider because it means that belief is more powerful than mere qualifications, and it is now widely accepted that the power of belief in one's self is an important factor in determining one's success in any chosen field, as the following article points out.

*Why England Can't Win a Shoot-Out—
England fails 'because the nation expects it.'*[15]

England footballers are bad at penalties because they are living up to a stereotype, psychologists say today.

Shoot-out failures, such as Gareth Southgate's against Germany in Euro 96 may happen because that is what the country expects, according to new research.

Success or failure at sport, at work or in school is not always due to ability or competence but simple self-belief, says the study.

---

15. *Daily Telegraph*, 22nd April 2008, reported by Roger Highfield.

The researchers say that low expectations, "the power of stereotypes," can mean poor performance. In the case of the England team, the expectation that they will lose a shoot-out, based on previous disasters, may now be a self-fulfilling prophecy.

The team has won only one of seven shoot-outs in major tournaments and defeats like the 1990 World Cup semi-final against West Germany, weigh heavily on the team.

"If you look at the performance of individuals in the England team it would appear that they are not particularly worse than the Germans," says Professor Alex Haslam, of the University of Exeter, who conducted the study with psychologists at the University of St. Andrews. "But when they play for England they are aware that others expect them to fail, just as the Germans know that others expect them to win, and that has an impact on their performance and will compromise it." The report, published in the magazine 'Scientific American Mind,' says that self-belief can improve sporting success by up to five per cent, as much as illegal performance-enhancing drugs.

So it seems self-evident that the beliefs we hold and the stereotypes we live up to, are possibly based on what we think others expect us to achieve—or not achieve, have a direct bearing on our ability to succeed. In essence, what we believe we are likely to expect, or what we believe others expect of us, has an effect on our ability and performance. This doesn't necessarily have to pertain to sport. It could relate to the personal, family, social and business areas of our lives.

Another example of the power of self-belief and how it can be used to improve and increase performance can be seen in the following article written by Joe Kolezynski for an on-line self-help magazine.

Joe Kolezynski is a well-respected individual. He has acted as a consultant to many famous self-help and motivational speakers, authors and trainers, including Anthony Robbins and Deepak Chopra. He holds a BBA degree in Accounting, an MBA in Finance, MA in Sports Counseling and a Ph.D. in Sports Psychology. He has also served as Sports Psychologist for the UCSD Golf Team. His article is as follows and makes for very interesting reading.

Belief, Self-Talk and Performance[16]
by
Joe Kolezynski. M.B.A., M.A.

One of the more frequently faced challenges experienced by athletes is that of how to improve their performance. They express frustration that they often possess identical, if not superior, physical attributes to their competition, yet they're consistently being out performed by that competition. In many of these cases the factor that separates their performance from the competitions has been found to be rooted in their belief as to their ability to outperform the competition. In other words they are operating with a limiting belief as to their athletic ability and level of performance they are capable of achieving. Yet it is well documented that an individual's core beliefs in any given area of their life will ultimately determine the reality they draw into their life—positive, negative or stagnant.

So how does one go about changing a limiting belief to a positive one—one that will result in improving your performance? It has been established by psychologists and neuroscientists that every person in the world carries on an ongoing dialog, or self-talk, of between 150 and 300 words a minute. This works out to between 45,000 and 51,000 thoughts a day. Most of our self-talk is harmless thoughts that serve our daily activities like, "I need to stop at the cleaners." The danger is when inner dialogue takes on a negative connotation such as, "I'll never be as good an athlete as he is," "I don't have the mental toughness to compete at this level," or "I'll never be that fast." The ongoing negative reinforcement created by habitual negative self-talk results in the creation of a limiting belief(s) that goes on to become self-fulfilling prophecy.

---

16. 'Belief, Self Talk and Performance' by Joe Kolezynski, *Self Help Magazine*: www.selfhelpmagazine.com/articles/sport/selftalk.html

Beliefs—positive or negative—are literally etched into our brain in comfortable grooves or neural pathways. Incoming data from our senses travel on these neural pathways on the way to interpretation in the brain. Therefore, if you desire to change an unresourceful/limiting belief into an empowering belief, you must rewire the negative neural track created in the brain.

This can be accomplished in precisely the same way the tracks were created: by using self-talk or, more specifically affirmations. An affirmation is a statement of fact or belief—positive or negative—that will lead toward the end result you expect. Anything that follows the phrase "I am," such as "I am a peak performance athlete" or "I am quick and agile," is an affirmation. The simplicity of affirmations often causes them to be overlooked. Nonetheless, affirmations are regularly used by professional athletes and successful business people.

The process for changing a limiting belief to a resourceful belief using affirmations is a simple one. First, identify the areas of your life which are not working to your satisfaction.

Next, write out the affirmations that represent things the way you desire them to be, they will be the vehicles for creating new resourceful/positive pathways.

Basic to formulating a new self-suggestion is that your affirmation is short and to the point—simple enough that a five-year old child will understand it —and is always stated in the positive. Further, your affirmation should be stated in the present tense—as if it has already happened, for example, "I am a strong athlete."

At the end of this chapter is an exercise in writing affirmations to help you devise a list of affirmations that can help you transform your life by helping your create new and more functional beliefs about yourself and your ability.

AFFIRMATIONS

> "It's the repetition of affirmations that leads to belief. And once that belief becomes a deep conviction, things begin to happen."
>
> Muhammad Ali

As you have just read affirmations can be very important components in manifesting positive change, yet some people find this hard to believe. However, these are probably the same people who are using negative and limiting affirmations that have resulted in them being in a position or situation that they are not happy with.

We, in fact, use affirmations all the time. We are always using them, and the more we use one, the more likely we are to repeat it—unless of course we recognise it, challenge it and replace it with a more functional one. Think about it! How many people do you know who regularly say things to themselves like: *"I'm stupid,"* *"I'm bad,"* *"I'm not worth caring for,"* *"I'm unlucky I love,"* *"I hate my job,"* *"I hate my life,"* etc.? These are negative affirmations that reinforce and promote negative belief systems. And you have met some of these people. Maybe you were one once?

The thing is, the constant repetition of negative affirmations will only lead to the individual finding the evidence they require in their experiences to self-justify their negative belief system. Its like going shopping and repeating a mental shopping list so that you will remember what to buy.

Affirmations, however, are not new things. They have been around for millennia. How many of you can now do mental maths simply because when you were in school you had to recite your times-tables over and over again in class. Those were affirmations. How many of you can recall nursery rhymes? That is simply because you were not only told it many times, you also possibly repeated it time and time again in your own head. They were learned through the process of affirmations. How many of you pray or recite mantras. These are affirmations.

If you draw your mind back to chapter three you can see the effect of thought and language on the fifty trillion cells that make up our body. We know that our language influences our physical and mental well being so wouldn't it make sense to use more positive affirmations than negative ones?

YOUR PAST IS NOT YOUR FUTURE

The reason why so many limiting beliefs are well established is that many people look to their past to create their future. In doing so they simply re-create their past. The major difference with most successful people, either in business, relationships and health, is that they constantly and consistently look to their future to capitalise on the possible opportunities that exist for them.

All possibilities and opportunities exist in our ability to look to the future and in using our imagination to change our focus of attention so that we draw into our lives only those things that we wish to draw in, to support our new world view.

YOU ARE FAR GREATER THAN YOU COULD POSSIBLY EVER IMAGINE

> *"The greatest discovery of my generation is that human beings, by changing their inner attitudes of their minds, can change the outer aspects of their lives."*
>
> William James

In chapter one you will have read the following passage taken from Nelson Mandella's inagural speech in 1994. Read it once more and this time as you do so think about yourself. Consider what beliefs you may possibly have that have stopped you from enjoying your life to the full, and then consider where those limiting beliefs possibly came from.

> *Our deepest fear is not that we are inadequate. Our deepest fear is that we are powerful beyond measure. It is our light, not our darkness, that most frightens us. We ask ourselves, who am I to be brilliant, successful, talented and fabulous? Actually, who are you NOT to be?*

You are a child of God. Your playing small doesn't serve the world. There's nothing enlightened about shrinking so that other people won't feel insecure around you. We were born to make manifest the glory that is within us. It's not just in some of us; it's in EVERYONE! And as we let our own light shine, we unconsciously give other people permission to do the same. As we are liberated from our own fear, our presence automatically liberates others!

Now you have done that stop for a moment and start deciding for yourself whether you still wish to believe those old limiting beliefs or whether, just like those great ancient thinkers, explorers and scientists of the past, you are now ready to throw away those dogmatic shackles of belief that have stopped you being who and what you want to be.

If you are then you can begin to do the exercise at the end of this chapter on affirmations.

EXERCISE—THE POWER OF AFFIRMATIONS

"I am the greatest, I said that even before I knew I was."
          Muhammad Ali

All this exercise requires is for you to:

1. Identify an area of your life (or work) that is not working to your satisfaction.

2. Write out the affirmation that will represent things the way you want them to be.

or

1. Identify a positive trait that you have and focus on it more, or

2. Identify a positive trait that you want to have and write it down as though you already have it.

What you need to do is make sure that you construct the affirmation in a positive tense, as you did in the reframing exercise in Chapter 2.

Also, write the affirmation in the present tense, as if you have already achieved it.

Remember, the golden key to writing and reciting affirmations is to keep them simple.

What is not working	Affirmation
I don't enjoy my job.	I have begun to notice more and more each day those things, no matter how small, that make me grateful for the fact that I have a job.
Life gets me down.	I am truly grateful for the fact that I have good health and that I find more and more things each day to be thankful for.
I want a better life	I always focus on the positive, which in doing so has brought into my life those things that help me improve my life for the better each day.
Positive Trait	**Affirmation**
Patience	I am truly patient. I have the capacity to remain calm in all situations.
Wealth	I am truly rich. Money comes to me in abundance. I have more wealth than I ever imagined possible.
Happiness	I am truly happy. Every day I experience situations, circumstances and events that bring joy into my life and a smile onto my face. Life is full of opportunities that lift my spirits every day.
Health	I am in good health. I experience improved health every day and I notice more how much better I become as each day passes.

CHAPTER 9.
STRESS

Stress is now an everyday word that we bandy about for anything and everything that seems to upset us. We are constantly informed about the constant pressure of living in a modern world and we see people all around us who seem to be suffering from this thing called stress.

In our modern, get-it-quick, immediate results, throw away society, change is happening faster and more frequently than ever before. The 'job-for-life' society that our parents lived in no longer applies to us. In our business and work life we now experience, downsizing, organisational re-organisation and re-allocation of job definitions in our workplaces.

A recent article entitled *'Slump gives City mental health crisis'* in the *London Evening Standard* on the 23rd June 2008 informed us that more city workers are suffering mental health problems because of extreme stress caused by the credit crunch. It stated that clinics serving the City of London are reporting a huge rise in calls from bankers and traders facing the threat of redundancy, and emergency help-lines are dealing with a record number of men at risk of suicide and women executives with eating disorders also apparently brought on by chronic stress.

According to the Health and Safety Executive's website (www.hse.gov.uk), *The 2006/7 Survey of Self-Reported Work-Related Illness* indicated that around 530,000 individuals in Britain believed they were experiencing work-related stress at a level that was making them ill. And, according to the *2007 Psychosocial Working Conditions Survey,* around 13.6% of all working individuals thought their job was very or extremely stressful.

The Health and Safety Executive has also, very kindly, provided us with a definition of work-related stress which is: *"The adverse reaction people have to excessive pressure or other types of demand placed on them."*

According to the report *"New Directions in Managing Employee Absence,"* released by the Chartered Institute of Personnel and

Development (CIPD) in 2007, stress, depression and anxiety are the second largest cause of lost workdays in the United Kingdom. The analysis shows that people suffering from depression took an average of 30 days off work per year, while those suffering from stress and anxiety took an average of 21 days off work. Another article that appeared in *Personnel Today* in October 2006 stated that stress is the biggest problem in the UK workplace.

Our private and personal lives are also different from what our parents experienced. Life seems to operate at a faster pace. Children in school are under pressure from an early age to achieve results in the interest of school league tables. We have more debt now than ever before in an attempt to keep up with the trappings of what modern society expects us to have, and the cost of living is increasingly making life hard for many on limited incomes. Our moral and ethical social codes of order are being replaced by more and more legislation in an attempt to stem the apparent rising tide of crime that is reported in our media every day. Many people live in fear within their own communities. And in our communities, surrounded by thousands of other people, many live their lives alone and in isolation.

As a result stress, and the effects of stress, have perhaps now become the number one problem of the twenty-first century.

STRESS HYPNOSIS?

But is it actually stress that we are suffering from, or are we being *hypnotised* into believing something without questioning it?

We are constantly being bombarded with lots of information about stress and the negative effects of it. As a result many organisations are now required by the Health and Safety Executive to undertake 'stress audits' to find out how much stress staff are experiencing at work. As a result of the audit the organisation finds out that it has a bigger stress problem then it actually thought it had, so the next solution is to bring in a 'stress consultant' to educate staff about the damaging effects of stress. Having now educated their staff on the dangers of being stressed, the staff have become even more stressed than before. Stress has increased! They have actually found out that they are suffering from stress that they didn't have before, and now they have been told, by a 'stress expert', that they may die prematurely from it! This creates even more stress and the member of staff, now more *educated* and more 'stress aware,' start to see evidence all around them of the negative aspects of stress as they attract and draw into their conscious awareness information to support the way they feel.

What we focus on we find more of!

In short, they find the reasons to support their belief that stress is bad for them, but what's worse is that they resign themselves to the fact that there is no hope. In other words, they genuinely believe that they have no control over their lives and it is this perceived lack of control that causes the problem. People have learned to be helpless.

WHAT ACTUALLY IS STRESS?

But what exactly is stress? Is stress the symptom or is stress the cause? Is stress something that is imposed on us, or is stress something we impose on ourselves. In short, stress has been blamed for being the symptom, the cause and the effect. As a result the word 'stress' has become the 'catch-all' definition for anything that makes us feel ill, bad or upset.

The first person to define an aspect of stress was Dr. Walter Cannon. He was the first to describe what he referred to as the *'fight or flight'* response in an article entitled *"The Role of Emotion in Disease."*[17] What Dr. Cannon discovered was that when a stressful event occurs, or is just perceived, the brain responds by triggering the release of specific hormones from the hypothalamus, the pituitary gland and the adrenal glands. The adrenal glands release a chemical called epinephrine, which is more commonly known as adrenaline. This in turn causes the sympathetic nerves, which

---

17. "The Role of Emotion in Disease" by W. B. Cannon, *Annals of Internal Medicine*, 9: 1453-1465, 1936.

are found in every organ and tissue in the body, to produce more adrenaline when they are stimulated by the initial release of adrenaline from the adrenal glands, to ready us for the violent action of fighting or flighting.

Dr. Hans Seyle was another pioneer in the field of stress and one of the first doctors to research the link between emotional stress and disease. What Dr. Seyle concluded was that emotions such as fear and anger also caused stimulation of the hypothalamus, the pituitary gland and the adrenal glands making our senses more alert and priming our bodies for the impending need to run or fight.

In addition to adrenaline, Seyle identified that we also produce cortisol, a human based steroid, that is designed to make us stronger to give us a better chance of survival if we have to run or fight. To give you some idea of the amount of cortisol generated we produce approximately fifty thousand molecules of cortisol from our adrenal glands for every one molecule of stress hormone that is secreted into the bloodstream by the hypothalamus when we are presented with, or when we perceive, a threat. This is what gives us our increased power and strength, which would come in very handy if we had to run away from a sabre-toothed tiger or fight a person who was attempting to kill us.

Now these physiological/biological changes are highly adaptable traits if we are faced with a possible life-threatening situation and we have all heard the stories of a woman being able to lift a car off a young boy trapped underneath it. Recently this phenomenon hit the press once again when a Royal Marine Commando lifted a section of a two-tonne Landrover to save the life of another Royal Marine trapped underneath it.

However, these physiological and biological changes can have severe consequences if they are not being used for their intended purposes within the correct context.

CONDITIONED ANGER, HOSTILITY, RAGE, DEPRESSION AND WORRY

Anger and hostility are conditioned-reflex responses. They are learned responses that have been conditioned and re-conditioned over time to become almost automatic responses. It is also like a trance state, the focus of attention in one area with to the exclusion of everything else.

If we are repeatedly exposed to anger and hostility in our environment, then we learn to become angry and hostile. It becomes the norm, and the more we become angry—the easier it is to become angry again in the future. It is a Pavlovian conditioned-reflex. In essence we build neurological networks in our brains that produce the habit of becoming angry and hostile. Eventually we become so good at it that we don't even know how we do it, so we end up believing that we have no control over it. To justify this apparent lack of control we end up developing beliefs such as; "*it just happens,*" "*that's just the way I am,*" to remove the responsibility from ourselves to do anything about it. We simply adopt our anger and hostility as another form of learned helplessness. In addition, our cells become addicted to the neuropeptides that have been consistently and frequently stimulating them every time we get angry and hostile. This results in our cells needing *their fix* every time they experience *withdrawal* from their drug. In simple terms, the pig is tethered and anger has become a phantom limb. (You will understand what I mean by this metaphor better when you read the next chapter on *Learned Helplessness.*)

DYING FOR ANGER

Scientific research has proved, many times over, that the emotion of anger, and other emotions like rage and hostility, have a detrimental effect on our hearts and our immune system. Anger, rage and hostility trigger the primitive flight and fight response, releasing more and more adrenaline and cortisol into our bodies. This, in turn, can cause blood sugar, insulin and cholesterol levels to rise and remain at high levels. Our primitive fight and flight response is therefore on continual high alert and looking for a reason to be triggered as opposed to only being used when required. In addition, the constant oversupply of cortisol can damage the hippocampus—the area of the brain used for storing and recalling memory.

Research done in Finland showed that anger and hostility are a major risk factor and predictor of coronary heart disease. The study showed that those who scored high on hostility scores were almost three times more likely to die from a heart-related illness. The study also highlighted that angry and hostile people have a higher risk of heart disease than that associated with smoking.

Other research also tends to highlight these facts:

A Harvard Medical School study of 1,623 heart attack survivors found that when subjects got angry during emotional conflicts, their risk of subsequent heart attacks was more than double that of those who remained calm.

A 20-year study of over 1,700 older men conducted by the Harvard School of Public Health found that worry about social conditions; health and personal finances all significantly increased the risk of coronary disease.

According to a Mayo Clinic study of individuals with heart disease, psychological stress was the strongest predictor of future cardiac events, such as cardiac death, cardiac arrest and heart attacks.

IMMUNE TO ANGER?

When we become angry and hostile we also affect the immune system. Now the immune system works in a delicate balance. In a healthy immune system the natural *killer* cells that the immune system possess work well, killing cancer cells, viruses and unhealthy bacteria whilst leaving the healthy cells alone. In essence, the natural killer cells of the immune system are its front-line troops, ready to destroy the enemy and protect the good. When we become angry or hostile the immune system becomes over-stimulated. In these circumstances the natural *killer* cells of the immune system are on constant alert and overdrive. What happens then is that once the enemy has been killed, the troops are still getting orders to kill, so they turn on the healthy cells and bacteria. This results in a depleted immune system that no longer has the defences to combat unhealthy cells, viruses and bacteria, leaving the individual vulnerable to attack from within.

PARASITIC THINKING

> *"Every man has inside himself a parasitic being who is acting not at all to his advantage."*
> William S. Burroughs

Parasitic wasps are the largest group of wasps in the world. They reproduce by laying their eggs on or inside another insect's egg, usually a caterpillar egg or larva that has been paralysed by it so that it remains alive. When the wasp larva eventually hatches from its egg, it gets food and nourishment by feeding on its host, which is still alive at the time. It first feeds on non-essential body tissues so as not to kill its food source too quickly, but eventually consumes the host completely. The fully-fed wasp larva then forms its own pupa, from which an adult parasitic wasp will emerge.

Anger and hostility, as well as depression and worry, are parasitical diseases of the mind that we invite into existence. They attach themselves to us on the inside, and are sculpted and formed by our own distorted view of the world or circumstances, and they grow larger the more we feed them more angry, hostile, depressed and worrying thoughts. Eventually they become self-actualised, having their own self-justifying purpose allowing them to eat away at us from the inside, just as dry-rot will eat away at wood, using us as food until they eventually consume us totally.

CAN IT EVER BE OK TO GET ANGRY OR SAD?

If by reading this book you have come to the conclusion that I am some inane-grinning, happy-smiley-faced, angelic, butter-wouldn't-melt-in-my mouth, evangelical preacher of laughter, you are wrong.

Yes my life has changed, in some ways very dramatically, but I am still human. I don't live a delusional existence. I am a married man with two teenage children, I run a business and I have to pay my bills, go to work and balance work and family just like everyone else. As a result I have times when I get angry and I have times when I get sad. Lets face it, you wouldn't be human if you didn't.

However, what is different is how I can now recognise when what I am doing is destructive and when it can be constructive. What I mean by that is if I get angry it is because something or someone has annoyed me—but what I do with it now is different to what I used to do with it.

I have learned to harness my anger and use it to my advantage, in the same way that a cowboy tames a wild horse so that he can ride it. I use anger as a means of motivation. If something makes me angry then I do something about it. But here's the golden key, what I do has to create a positive outcome. There has to be a benefit in what I do as opposed to a drawback.

Do I ever get sad? Yes of course I do. Again, I wouldn't be human if I didn't. If I have a row with a loved one and it has upset me, or I have said or done something to upset them, I'll very possibly feel sad. Sadness and anger are emotional barometers that let us know when something isn't right. Without anger and sadness we wouldn't have the ability to provide the contrast required to distinguish right from wrong. However, we also have the choice to choose our response, and what I do is choose how I deal with those emotions, and I choose not to let my emotions have total control over me. I don't self-justify my emotional state by finding more to be angry or sad about. I deal with it, and put things back into perspective. I let it go and move forward.

PERCEPTUAL BLINDNESS

In Richard Wiseman's book, *Did you spot the Gorilla?*[18], he describes an experiment designed by Harvard psychologist Daniel Simons to study the psychology of vision. The thirty-second film consists of six basketball players, three wearing white T-shirts and three in

---

18. *Did You Spot the Gorilla?* by Richard Wiseman, Arrow Books, Limited (2004), ISBN 0-09-946643-0

black T-shirts. The aim of the exercise is to count only the amount of passes that the team in white make whilst ignoring the team in black. Halfway through the film a man wearing a gorilla costume walks in between the players, stops right in the middle of the screen, and beats his chest whilst looking straight at the camera, and then walks off.

At the end of the film everyone who has been watching the film are asked how many passes the team in white made. They are then asked if they saw anything unusual during the exercise. Astonishingly, very few people saw the gorilla.

Once the film clip is re-run the viewers are astounded that they missed the gorilla. Many people actually believe that the clip is not the same.

I have actually used this exercise myself and when I do I add a bit of pressure to the group by making the exercise a competition. For example, I will divide the group into two groups, or make it a competition between men and women, to see who will get the correct amount of passes. The primary aim of doing so is to create a bit of pressure so that each person is highly focussed on counting the passes. As a result, they miss the gorilla!

When we become frustrated, angry, depressed or hostile we also tend to focus our attention in a more polarised way. As a result, we get caught up in detail rather than being able to see the bigger picture. Because of this we often fail to see the obvious solutions that are right in front of our eyes. In essence, we become unintentionally blind to the gorilla literally thumping its chest in front of us.

This happens because of the way our minds work. If we look at our brains we can see that they are primarily made up of two distinct, yet identical hemispheres—a left one and a right one.

What neurologists and neuropsychologists now know is that our left hemisphere is more serious and analytical, whereas our right hemisphere is more creative, has the ability to see the bigger picture and generally likes to have a laugh.

When we are under pressure we become more polarised in our focus and so we end up engaging the left hemisphere more than the right one. So we are likely to repeat patterns that we have used before and not look for alternative or more creative options.

Consider this, have you ever had a problem that you have spent absolutely ages trying to figure out, or ever forgotten something that you really would like to remember, only to find that the more you think about it—the harder it becomes to resolve the problem or recall what was forgotten? Eventually you give up and go to bed, only to wake up in the middle of the night having resolved or recalled the very thing you had spent all day thinking about?

All the time you were trying to resolve or remember something, you were using the brain's left hemisphere and the more frustrated you became, the more polarised your thinking became—making it less likely for you to find the solution. The minute you began to relax, you switched into right hemispheric dominance. As a result, your thinking became more creative and your recall and ability to resolve the issue improved, resulting in the solution you were seeking to just pop into your mind.

So next time you lose your keys, instead of rushing around your house in a state of panic, sit down, close your eyes and relax. You'll probably find them more quickly.

Taking a leaf out of Professor Wiseman's book, how many of us miss opportunities in the form of gorillas everyday, simply because we are too focussed or 'stressed.'

MECHANICAL STRESS?

The concept of stress, in terms of how its principles are applied today, derives very much from engineering terms Dr. Hans Seyle used in his research. This is because he wanted to transfer the engineering model of *stress*, the force that is applied to an object, and *strain*, the deformation that an object experiences under stress, to the study of living things.

Hans Selye's idea therefore, was to define *stress* as the external event, and *strain* as the way the body responded to it. Unfortunately, confusion has occurred since then with regard to the use of the words 'stress and strain,' which has led to the word *stress* being referred to something that exists in its own right. The word *stress* has now become distorted and can now be viewed as the existence and the cause itself, dependent on the view of the person experiencing it and/or the perception of the person providing the professional advice.

For example, lets say I have a friend at work that is experiencing an increased workload, which is placing additional demands on his limited time resources. This additional *strain* on his resources (time) could be regarded as *'additional workplace stress.'* Now, as a result of this increased workload my friend experiences the emotional states: frustration and/or anger. This could also be regarded as *'workplace stress.'* On the way home my friend is caught in a traffic jam which means he will be late in arriving home, and may not get back in time to watch his favourite television show. Could this be referred to as a form of *'stress?'* As a result of the traffic delays he got angry and frustrated, someone jumped the traffic cue and cuts him up which *'stresses him out'* even more. This causes feelings of injustice and increased anger, or road rage. Is this a form of *'emotional stress?'* On arriving home, he is so wound-up that he decides to go down to the gym to *'de-stress.'* So he goes and has a heavy workout, placing his body under physical stress and strain. However, afterwards he feels good about it. On arriving back home, he winds down by having a few glasses of wine or a beer to *'relax'* or *'de-stress'* himself further because of the stressful day he has had so far. The next morning on waking up, he thinks of the *'stressful day ahead'* and is not looking forward to it. So he decides to take the day off. However, this is not the first time he has done this. In order to cover himself, he goes to see his GP who asks him what is wrong. On hearing the tales of woe about increased workload, how much he hates his job, travelling etc., the GP decides that he is suffering from *'stress'* and signs him off for a few weeks whilst also prescribing a course of pills. Now off work for two weeks, my friend begins to worry about going back, about what his manager may or may not say to him on his return to work, what his work-colleagues will think of him, the amount of work piling up whilst he is away from work, and the list goes on causing him increased levels of anxiety, or *'stress.'*

In short, the word 'stress,' and it's various current definitions, are too wide ranging, and as such can be misleading, and incorrect when used out of context.

STRESS PHOBIA

According to Angela Patmore, who undertook twenty-five years of study into the subject of stress, people are suffering from 'stress phobia' and not stress itself. A phobia being defined as: *"a persistent abnormal fear or dislike of something."*[19]

In Patmore's book, *The Truth About Stress*[20], she argues that the stress management industry seems to help promote the fact that stress exists (in its currently defined terms) and that it is also very bad for us. In defining the term, the stress management industry has created a dogma that is causing many millions of people to believe that they have become victims of a 'disease,' which they further believe they have no control over. This causes individuals to live in conditions of learned helplessness. More on this in the next chapter.

IT'S ALL ABOUT PERCEPTION

The difference between whether a situation is stressful or not, whether we become angry or upset, whether we choose to worry or not, lies in the perception of the meaning given to the event—not the event itself.

For example, I have a good friend that hates going to parties or having surprise parties thrown for him. If he has to attend a party, he will worry about attending long before even attending the event. In short it is his perception of the event that triggers the response.

In Don Colbert's book, *Deadly Emotions*[21], he relates the following conversation he had with a person to illustrate the point:

> A person recently said to me, "I don't get it. On Friday, I get up absolutely exhausted and I go through my day in

---

19. *Oxford English Dictionary.*
20 *The Truth about Stress* by Angela Patmore, Atlantic Books (2006), ISBN: 1-84354-235-8.
21 *Deadly Emotions: Understand the Mind-Body-Spirit Connection That Can Heal or Destroy You* by Don Colbert, M.D., Thomas Nelson (10/2003), ISBN 978-0785267430.

great anticipation that the weekend is coming. I collapse into bed at night, grateful that I can sleep in and don't have to go to work the next day. But then on Saturday morning I awaken earlier than I do on a workday. I dive into projects around the house and then do a round of shopping errands, perhaps taking time out for morning coffee with a friend and then going to a late-afternoon movie and dinner with friends. At the end of the day I've accomplished just as much or more than I do on a workday, I'm just as much on the go, I talk to just as many people and get just as many or more tasks done, and I'm not at all tired at the end of the day. What's with that?"

Don Colbert replied: "*You don't believe Saturday is a workday. It's all about perception. You perceive Monday, Tuesday, Wednesday, Thursday and Friday as being about work, and you believe work means effort, responsibility, a tight schedule, intense focus, and all kinds of other things that you perceive are difficult. You perceive that Saturday is about play, and you believe play means fun, friends, shopping, and 'playing house.' What you believe, and what you perceive, determines how much stress you have, and the amount of stress determines how tired you feel at the end of the day.*"

My friend John Steadman and I don't go to work—we go on holiday. We go to play. We always try to see the funny side of things and have a good time. Recently while away on business we checked into a hotel to be greeted by a less than friendly receptionist who said: "*Business or pleasure.*" Not wanting to miss out when given the choice we replied, "*Pleasure please.*" This seemed to annoy the receptionist who, without lifting her head up to look at us responded, "*No. Are you here on business or pleasure?*" to which we both looked at each other, nodded in agreement, and replied, "*Yep, definitely pleasure please.*" Less than happy with our response she said, "*Your obviously here on business so I'll put you down for business. Have a nice day.*"

Now I'm not being judgemental here but who was in an emotional state of fight and flight? Not hard to figure out is it?

When I was younger I used to play a lot of sport and went down to the gym every day, sometimes three times a day. Now I didn't find this at all stressful. In fact it was more of a social occasion. I'd meet up with friends, there'd be some healthy rivalry and banter, and we lived by the motto of *"Work hard, play hard."* We used to ache after our sessions in the gym. Our muscles used to be sore, but the secret was that we enjoyed it. It wasn't at all stressful. Now, ask me to do some gardening or go shopping, a much less demanding activity, or go to a function that I don't want to be at and I'll probably put my body and mind under more emotional stress than a three-hour heavy gym session.

When it comes to the real issue of what stress is all about, what we choose to believe and what we choose to perceive is the golden key. This is because what we choose to believe will act as a self-fulfilling prophecy that will make us focus only on those things that we need to focus on to make our beliefs into realities.

However, by becoming too focused on proving something to be true—we may well be missing other, more obvious facts that are right in front of our eyes, which, if only noticed, could allow us to lead us to live a much more relaxed and fulfilling life.

CHAPTER 10.
LEARNED HELPLESSNESS

"From the point of view of public health education, one of the greatest flaws in the stress industry is that it fails to distinguish between arousal and resignation. Arousal and resignation lie at the opposite ends of the emotional spectrum when it comes to defining stress, yet the majority of the research uses the same word, 'stress,' for both emotional extremes, which has led to the confusion of two very different responses."

From *The Truth About Stress*
by Angela Patmore

Resignation or 'learned helplessness' is a response designed to protect an animal that is about to become prey from the pains of imminent death. The 'resignation' response floods the brain with opiate-like substances to deaden the fear and pain of impending slaughter, closing down the immune system, which is no longer required. An example of this was when the zoo-owner John Aspinall fell into a bear pit and was almost killed by an angry bear. He reported that as he lay on the ground in the bear's enclosure, expecting to suffer a horrible death, he *"was overwhelmed by a sudden strange sense of relief and tranquillity,"* and surmised that this must be some natural mechanism that enables prey animals to face painful and terrifying death. What Mr Aspinall actually experienced was the state of the resignation aspect of the survival response being used in the correct context.

However, outside of these types of situations, the resignation response is maladaptive. For example we have people in our society who have 'resigned' themselves to the fact that they have no control over their environment and as such have learned to be helpless.

IVAN PAVLOV AND THE CONDITIONED REFLEX

Ivan Pavlov was a Russian physiologist, psychologist and physician who was awarded a Nobel prize in 1904 and who is possibly best known for his experiments into the 'conditioned reflex,' known as 'Pavlov's dog.'

What Pavlov observed was a dog salivates when it encounters food. However, Pavlov also noticed that sometimes the dogs also salivated when no food was in sight. On closer observation he deduced that the dogs were reacting to the lab coats worn by the staff that fed them. Basically, every time the dogs were served food, the person who served the food was wearing a lab coat. Therefore, the dogs reacted as if food was on its way and produced saliva whenever they saw a lab coat.

What Pavlov then did was to set up an experiment whereby he created an 'associative stimulus' response by linking the sound of a bell with the feeding of the dogs. Each time the dogs were due to be fed, a bell would be rung. Over time the dogs associated the sound of the bell with being fed and would produce saliva in response to the sound, even though no food was in sight. In short, the dogs had been 'conditioned' to the sound of the bell and the anticipation of being fed.

Pavlov discovered that external environmental events (such as the sound of a bell or the sight of a lab coat) could, through repetition or consistent exposure, trigger a reflex (salivation). He called this the 'conditioned reflex,' and the process whereby dogs or humans learn to connect a stimulus to a reflex is called conditioning. In NLP terms this type of conditioning is referred to as 'anchoring.'

Many years later, in a research study undertaken by Martin Seligman, dogs were conditioned according to Pavlov's methods. The dogs were placed in one compartment of a box that had two compartments, separated by a low wall that the dogs could easily jump over. What Seligman then did was to expose the dogs to two external stimuli, a high-pitched tone and a brief electrical shock so that the dogs would soon associate the tone with the electrical shock. What Seligman expected to see was that the dogs, on hearing the tone would soon learn to jump over the wall into the second compartment to avoid the painful shock.

However, on hearing the tone all the dogs did was simply lie down and whimper. They didn't even try to escape. What the dogs had done was to accept that nothing they could do mattered, so why bother. In short they had learned to he helpless.

What Seligman concluded as a result of his experiment was that the dogs that had learned to become helpless displayed many of the same psychological features of depressed human beings.[22]

However, if we can learn to be helpless—can we unlearn it?

VILAYANUR RAMACHANDRAN AND LEARNED PARALYSIS

In a talk hosted by TED.com in 2007, the respected neurologist, Vilayanur Ramachandran, addressed the complex circuitry that is set up in the brain by considering a syndrome called phantom-limb syndrome. For those of us unfamiliar with what a phantom limb is, it is when, an arm or a leg is amputated but the person still feels the presence of their missing limb. That missing limb that is still felt is known as a 'phantom.'

In his experiments into phantom limbs, Ramachandran found that about half of the patients with phantom limbs claimed that they could move the missing limb. He recounted stories of patients telling him that their phantom arms would pat someone on the shoulder, answer the phone when it rang, wave goodbye etc., and that these were very vivid sensations for the amputee.

Now these patients are not delusional. They know that their arm is not there, but nevertheless the experience is a compelling sensory one for them. However, in half the patients, this doesn't seem to happen. They experience a paralysed phantom limb. In a paralysed phantom arm for example, the limb is fixed in a clenched spasm and is excruciatingly painful. The patient believes that if only they could move it—the pain would be relieved.

---

22. *Learned Helplessness: A Theory for the Age of Personal Control* by Christopher Peterson Steven F. Maier, Martin E. P. Seligman, Oxford University Press (1995), ISBN: 978-0195044676.

Now why would a phantom limb be paralysed? When Ramachandran looked at the case sheets, he found that the original arm was paralysed because of a peripheral nerve injury; the actual nerve supplying the arm was severed, actually cut because of an accident. So, in these cases, the patient had an injured arm that was painful and in a sling for a few months or a year prior to amputation and then, in a misguided attempt to relieve the pain in the arm, the surgeon amputated the arm. However, in this effort to relieve the patient of the pain, what actually occurred was that although the physical arm was now gone, the pain still remained. What has happened is that the pain has been carried over so now the patient experiences a phantom arm with the same pain as before.

Now the patient could see that they do not have an actual arm anymore, but nevertheless, they still continued to experience the pain as if their arm were still there. This is known as *Phantom limb syndrome* which is a serious clinical problem and leads some patients to become depressed, with some even driven to suicide.

So why does this happen? When the actual arm was intact but paralysed, the brain was sending commands to the arm saying, "Move," but was getting visual feedback showing the arm not moving. Over time these commands and feedback eventually end up getting wired into the circuitry of the brain, and this is what Ramachandran refers to as 'learned paralysis.'

In short, because of the contrasting feedback generated between the command to move the arm, and the visual feedback showing the arm not moving, the brain 'learns' that the arm can't move. Then, when the arm is amputated, this 'learned paralysis' carries over into the person's body image and subsequently into the phantom limb.

So, what Ramachandran wanted to know was how to help these patients? He wanted to know how they could 'unlearn' this process of 'learned paralysis,' so that they could be relieved of the excruciating pain in their phantom limbs.

His idea was a revolutionary, yet a brilliantly simple one. Ramachandran wanted to know what would happen if he sent a command to the phantom to move but gave the patient visual feedback that the phantom is obeying the brain's commands by actually moving. Would this relieve the phantom pain? Well Ramachandran hit on a way of doing this for only three dollars. Yes, three dollars.

What he did was to create what he refers to as a 'mirror box,' which is basically a box with a mirror in the middle so that when the patient inserts both arms into each side of the box (either side of the mirror) they see not only their good arm but also an image of their phantom arm, which is really only the reflection of their good arm in the mirror. The reflection of their good arm provides the patient with a vivid visual representation of a resurrected phantom limb that normally cannot be seen.

When the patient is then told to wiggle their fingers, or move the hand of their real (good) arm, whilst looking at the reflective image representing where their phantom arm should be, they get a visual impression that their phantom limb is moving. As obvious as this sounds, the astonishing thing that Ramachandran found was that the patient claimed to actually see their phantom arm moving, and in doing so the pain/clenching spasm was released.

However, when this experiment was repeated with the patient's eyes closed—no release of pain was experienced. Yet, when the patient opened their eyes to see the visual image of their resurrected phantom arm moving—all pain was once again relieved. This proved to Ramachandran the existence of 'learned paralysis' and the critical role of visual input in relieving phantom limb pain.

In one experiment, a patient who took the mirror box home to practice for two weeks, phoned Ramachandran to tell him that the phantom arm he had been experiencing for over ten years, and the pain associated with it, had disappeared completely. After only two weeks of using the mirror box to provide virtual visual feedback of a moving limb, the clenched phantom limb and all of the pain associated with it, had gone for good.

This lead Ramachandran into realising that other kinds of paralysis, such as stroke, may have a component of 'learned paralysis' to it, which can be overcome by the use of virtual visual feedback.

His technique has been tried on dozens of groups all over the world, and is proving invaluable in the treatment of phantom limb pain, as well as in stroke rehabilitation.

Now if this works for Phantom limb sufferers and stroke victims, surely it must work in other areas of our lives. For example, if we can generate visual feedback into our minds that we already possess certain character traits, or that we have already become successful, or that we are well and have overcome a certain illness, for example, can't that have a positive generative effect on us as well? The answer would appear to be, "Yes!"

THE PIG AND THE TWIG

As I listened to the talk by Vilayanur Ramachandran, I was reminded of another very entertaining talk given by Chris Moon some years previously at a conference in Wales. Chris was blown up while supervising a land mine clearance in Mozambique in 1995, losing his right leg and right arm. He survived only through his sheer determination and since has run numerous marathons, including the punishing 137-mile Marathon des Sables across the Sahara desert, raising money for charity along the way.

Chris explained that one day while convalescing in either Cambodia or Mozambique (forgive me, Chris, if your reading this, as I can't remember where exactly it was) he looked out of his window to see a very large pig tethered by a piece of twine or string to a small twig that was sticking out of the ground.

Now this amused Chris as he could see that the pig was obviously big enough and strong enough to simply pull the twig out of the ground and escape, but it didn't. Chris wondered why.

The next time someone he knew entered his hut, he asked why the pig didn't simply pull the twig out of the ground and escape. He was told that when the pig was a very small piglet, it was tethered to the twig in exactly the same way. As a small piglet, the animal didn't then possess enough size or strength to be able to pull the twig out of the ground and escape. So try as it might the twig and twine was strong enough to keep the piglet tethered and prevented it from escaping. Now everyday the piglet was re-attached to the twig by the twine, and everyday the piglet tired to escape, and everyday the piglet learned that no matter how hard it tried—it couldn't break free of it's twig and twine prison. Eventually the piglet grew into a large pig, and as it grew—it eventually accepted that it cannot break free from the twig. So now, although the fully-grown pig has the size, strength and the capability to break free—it has learned from numerous previous attempts as a small piglet that it cannot. It has learned to be helpless. So everyday, when the large fully-grown pig is tethered to its twig, it simply resigns itself to the fact that it is impossible to escape. In essence, the pigs own belief is what keeps it tethered—not the twig and twine!

In Geoff Thompson's book, *The Elephant and the Twig*[23], Geoff described how he was watching a documentary about how, in some parts of the world, fishermen caught crabs. He explains how they use a basket with a lid on the top just big enough for the crabs to climb through. Once a couple of crabs have crawled into the basket, the fishermen take the lid off and eventually the basket fills up with more crabs. Yet, in spite of the fact that there is no lid to keep the crabs in—none of the crabs manage to escape. The reason is because every time one crab tries to escape, the other crabs pull it back in again.

Now I am sure that crabs do not intentionally intend to prevent one of their own from escaping to freedom. They are probably acting out of some conditioned survival instinct. But it does make me wonder, it makes me wonder whether some people realise how their words and actions actually prevent other people from achieving their full potential in life. This isn't to say that their intention is wrong or bad. On the contrary, their intention may be in the other person's best interests. However, sometimes we have to let people go. We have to allow them to be free to make their own decisions and not drag them down because we think we know best.

---

23. *The Elephant and the Twig: The Art of Positive Thinking* by Geoff Thompson, Summersdale Publishers (12/2006), ISBN: 978-1840242645.

The reality is that conditioning is taking place all of the time, whether we notice it or not. Advertisers use this type of conditioning to get you to link their products with something or someone that creates a positive association that will hopefully make you buy their product.

Therefore, we can become conditioned and learn to be helpless or we can condition ourselves to success. The choice is ours.

CHAPTER 11.
HAPPINESS NOW

If I were to offer you an opportunity to improve your chances of living longer, to immediately feel better about yourself, and to improve your overall general health and well-being, that was totally free—didn't cost you anything, was readily available, an unlimited resource that would never run out—would you be interested?

You should be. Think about it, why do you work? Isn't one primary reason to improve the quality of your life or the lives of those you care for, so that you all can all live a happier life? If so, will being unhappy at work, and continually doing something that you believe makes you unhappy, help you achieve that goal? Seems to me that is the same dichotomy as attempting to achieve virginity by continually making love!

The fact is, happiness is not a destination or objective, and it's not something we eventually arrive at. It's something we do. It's an attitude towards life. It is our relationship to the way we feel about life, not to the way life makes us feel. In short happiness is something that you can achieve right now—if you want to.

The reality is that we become addicted to nothing more than our emotional state, and, as we have already discovered, our minds will generate the very chemicals we need to satisfy our emotional addiction, whatever it may be; anger, depression, sadness, victim-mentality, or joyful, happy, positive, upbeat, etc. If you need to feel bad about something, your brain will produce the neuropeptides to satisfy that emotional craving, and if you need to feel good about something, your brain will produce the neuropeptides necessary to satisfy that emotional craving. You hold the key to decide what chemicals you wish to flood your body with. The choice is actually yours. Think of it this way. Some people have a custard pie in one hand and a toxic, shit-filled pie in the other, and they choose to smack themselves in the face regularly with a pie full of crap, possibly even stating that they had no choice or control in the matter! Ever heard or used the expression *"life is shit"*—think about what you're flooding your body with and smacking yourself in the face with every time you say it!

WHAT WE FOCUS ON WE GET MORE OF!

Now what is interesting is that some of you who have read the previous paragraphs may possibly have immediately dismissed it as being 'too good to be true.'

But what if it were true? The fact is whatever you thought about in relation to the above paragraphs is simply down to your own focus of attention, or to put it another way, you've only looked for those things which your mind and senses expect to find. That's why for some the glass is half-full and for others half-empty. Furthermore, how you felt about what you have just read will have a direct effect on the chemicals you generate and choose to flood your body with.

There is now an abundance of research that proves that being happy is good for your health. For example, Dr Derek Cox, the Director of Public Health at Dumfries and Galloway NHS, suspects that for decades health professionals have been missing a big trick in improving the health of the nation. He summed this up recently when he said:

> *We've spent years saying that giving up smoking could be the single most important thing that we could do for the health of the nation. And yet there is mounting evidence that happiness might be at least as powerful a predictor, if not a more powerful predictor than some of the other lifestyle factors that we talk about in terms of cigarette smoking, diet, physical activity and those kind of things.*
>
> *If you are happy you are likely in the future to have less in the way of physical illness than those who are unhappy.*

SMILE YOURSELF FIT!

What is also interesting is that people tend to think that if they are physically well they will be happier as a result. However, it actually works other way round! The true fact is that if you are happy you are much more likely to be in better health!

Andrew Steptoe, the British Heart Foundation Professor of Psychology at University College London, has found that happier people also have greater protection against things like heart disease and stroke.

> "We know that stress which has bad effects on biology, leads to those bad changes as far as health is concerned," said Mr. Steptoe. "What we think is happening is that happiness has the opposite effect and has a protective effect on these same biological pathways."

Now I know this sounds simple, but adopting a more positive physical state changes our mental state. In a study undertaken by the University of California, they took people suffering from manic depression and made them change their facial expressions on a daily basis. The subjects were asked to smile on an ongoing basis. Now these are people that normally need drugs to change the way they feel and manage their emotional states, yet not one of them were able to feel depressed when they kept smiling. Some of them even began to manage the depressive aspects of the disorder themselves by smiling for 20 minutes at a time for no reason. This resulted in the subjects, developing new habits that made them feel great whenever they wanted to.

TALK YOURSELF INTO OLD AGE!

Research in the United States has also suggested a possible link between happiness and a long life. A study of nuns in Milwaukee examined the diaries of one intake of the Sisters of Notre Dame when they joined the convent back in the 1930s. As part of the study, the researchers counted the number of times the Sisters used positive and negative words in their diary entries. Some were brimming with joyful thoughts while others were a bit gloomy. This was enough for the modern-day researchers to divide the intake of Sisters into "happy nuns" and "not so happy nuns."

What the study showed was that after joining the order, the lives of the Sisters were almost exactly similar: the same food, same work, same routine—but this did not equate to the same life expectancy. Among the less positive nuns, two thirds died before their 85th birthday. Among the happy nuns, 90% were still alive. On average the happiest nuns lived about nine years longer than the unhappy nuns.

LAUGHTER IS THE BEST MEDICINE

> *"Laughter is inner jogging."*
> Norman Cousins

The most famous story of laughter as medicine has to be that of Norman Cousins. Cousins had been the editor of the Saturday Review for over thirty years when one day in 1964 he returned home from a meeting in Moscow experiencing severe joint pain and a fever. Eventually he was diagnosed with *ankylosing spondylitis*, a collagen illness that attacks the connective tissues of the body, which was most likely due to exposure to metal poisoning.

Cousin's, however, was not too convinced and had some reservations about the diagnosis. As a result he began to research the effects of negative emotions and stress on the body and what he found was that negative emotions could be harmful to the body and that stress could be detrimental to the immune system. He figured out for himself that if negative emotions were detrimental to health, then positive emotions should improve health. He was also concerned that the high doses of painkillers that he had been prescribed were possibly also likely to be harmful to his body. This motivated him to prescribe himself a medication of a different sort.

What Cousins did was to hire the services of a nurse who would read him funny and humorous stories, and he would watch Marx Brothers movies to make him laugh. His strategy proved to be effective and what he found was that laughter relieved his pain and also helped him sleep. As a result, and within a relatively short period of time, he was able to come off of all of the painkillers and sleeping pills that he had been prescribed.

Although his claims initially received quite a bit of criticism, it was finally acknowledged in the 1989 *Journal of the American Medical Association*, that laughter therapy could help to improve the quality of life for patients with chronic illnesses, and that laughter has an immediate symptom-relieving effect and can even help boost the immune system.

Since Cousins, numerous other independent medical studies have now shown that laughter boosts levels of endorphins, the body's natural painkillers, and suppresses the levels of stress hormones in our system.

Now this is not necessarily a new phenomenon. In France in the fourteenth century, the healing power of humour had already been generally accepted as a benefit by the medical fraternity. This is illustrated by the writing of Henri de Mondeville (1260-1320) an important French surgeon of the time:

> "Let the surgeon take care to regulate the whole regimen of the patient's life for joy and happiness, allowing his relatives and special friends to cheer him, and by having someone tell him jokes."

THE POWER OF LOVE

Referring once again to Viktor Frankl's book, *Man's Search for Meaning*, there comes a point in the book where Frankl recalls a thought he had which became a defining moment in his life. He recounts the experience as follows:

> *A thought transfixed me: for the first time in my life I saw the truth as it is set into song by so many poets, proclaimed as the final wisdom by so many thinkers. The truth—that love is the ultimate and highest goal to which man can aspire. Then I grasped the meaning of the greatest secret that human poetry and human thought and belief have to impart: The salvation of man is through love and in love.*

The power of love is now a medically recognised fact. Research has shown that a hug from a partner cuts blood pressure and your heart rate and wounds take longer to heal when the patient has been involved in an argument with a loved one. Research has also shown that people who feel unloved are more likely to die and a study of 17,000 Swedes found the lonely had four times the risk of sudden death.

In the Daily Mail on Monday, 23rd June 2008 an article entitled *'Girl of three saved by the power of her twin sister's love'* illustrated this fact clearly. Doctors treating a three-year-old girl for a cancerous brain tumour decided it would be beneficial to bring the girls twin sister into the treatment plan. The sisters had only spent one night apart from each other since birth, and the Doctors thought that having the girl's twin there would provide additional sisterly support. At the expert's suggestion, the girl's sister spent every available moment at her side, bringing in picnics and sleeping next to her on a camp bed. This turned an ordeal into an adventure for the three year-old, and her cancer went into remission. The mother of the two girls said that her sister was the best medicine she could have asked for, and also commented how the three-year-old had gained much more strength and support from her twin's presence.

Focussing on the positive and generating healthy emotions are the best medicine. The more powerful the emotion, the greater the dosage. That is why love is so powerful.

JUST DON'T DO IT!

The easiest way to not get stressed, therefore, is simply not to do it! If you consider that our minds work through the process of neuro-associative learning (read Chapter 4 on the *Groove Theory of Habitual Behaviour*) we can begin to understand that the more we do something, the more likely we are to repeat it. In other words, we develop behavioural patterns or habits based on repetition. Eventually we don't even know how we do stuff; we just accept we do it. Then we believe that we have no control over it—because we don't know why we do it. Some people even support their belief with the use of metaphorical language so that they don't have to abandon their habits with sayings such as *"You can't teach an old dog new tricks,"* and this in turn can lead to a state of 'learned helplessness'.

However, simply adopting new ways of thinking can break this cycle of learning. In other words, you can cut a new groove.

MANAGING YOUR ULTRADIAN RHYTHMS: THE BUCKET PRINCIPLE

Research has shown that the mind and body have their own pattern of rest and alertness, with one predominant cycle that occurs approximately every ninety minutes. This cycle is known as the 'Ultradian Rhythm.'

What happens in this ninety-minute period is that our mind stops thinking about external events and begins to focus on internal events. You have probably noticed this when people 'switch-off' and start 'day-dreaming.' At this point it becomes difficult for people to maintain concentration or focus on what they are supposed to be focussing on. As a result if they attempt to work through it they may end up making more mistakes as their minds become more focussed under pressure. If we ignore this natural rhythm, we become less productive. What this rhythm requires is a twenty-minute break every ninety minutes. This is the body's own natural stress-control mechanism.

Unfortunately, many people ignore the messages that it is time to relax and instead they drive themselves on, fuelled by another cup of coffee or caffeine drink to keep them going. After a while this behaviour can result in an individual overriding their body's natural rhythmic system designed for stress management.

To illustrate this try to imagine a bucket that's empty, and let's imagine that the emptiness equals tolerance, or capacity to undertake productive work. At the start of each ninety-minute cycle that's where we are. As we progress through the first forty-five minutes of the cycle we take on work and in doing so use up part of our personal resource or capacity. In essence our bucket is half-full, but that's not an issue as we still have half a bucket of productivity left. At the end of the ninety minutes, however, our bucket is full and needs emptying—otherwise it will overflow. We cannot continue trying to put more in it when we have used up all of the available capacity.

It is at this stage that we need to take a twenty-minute break. The purpose of the twenty-minute break is to empty the bucket, and this is an important thing to do as this helps our mind and body replenish our immune system. If our immune system becomes depleted, then it becomes less effective in fighting illness and so leaves us open to sickness or disease.

Think of it this way. Let's say you had a bank account and all you did was draw on it without making any deposits. If you continued to do this, then the bank would freeze your account and take action to stop you spending more than you could afford. Your body works the same way. Ever finished work and then fallen asleep on the couch at home? Ever had a break or a holiday away from work and ended up catching a cold or getting a sore throat? That's your body making you take time out to rest. At the more extreme end, it can enforce rest by hospitalising you.

This is why some organisations are now promoting 'power naps' at work, and this is not a new phenomenon. People have been using them for years. Winston Churchill, Margaret Thatcher, Thomas Edison and Salvador Dali are some of the proponents of its use, and in certain Mediterranean countries, to have a 'siesta' is considered normal.

Now I know what some of you will be saying. There is no way I can just 'nod-off' for twenty minutes at work and I can't stop every ninety minutes for a twenty-minute break! I have too much work to do and my boss will wonder what on earth I'm up to. Another way to manage this is to take shorter breaks more often. For example, health and safety regulations now require staff to take regular breaks away from their computer screens so this can be combined with 'emptying your bucket.'

These shorter breaks are even consistent with current thinking in the use of meditation. Many believe that to achieve 'inner peace' you need to spend hours in a meditative state. Well that may be so if you wish to become a Buddhist monk, but not so practical if you wish to lead a normal everyday life. Taking shorter meditative and relaxation breaks has now proved to be just as effective as sitting in a meditative state for hours. So a few minutes every hour or so can be enough to generate the state we need to empty our buckets.

A great thing about recharging your batteries is that you can do it anywhere, and some of you possibly already do. I bet some of you fall asleep on the train to and from work but somehow, almost miraculously, manage to wake up at your stop.

CONTROL YOUR BREATHING: PROGRESSIVE MUSCULAR RELAXATION

Progressive muscular relaxation is another way of countering pressure and is used by many sporting athletes the world over. All it involves is breathing, something anyone can do.

To do this exercise sit in a comfortable chair. Place your feet flat on the floor and place your hands on your abdomen. As you breathe try to breathe deep into your abdomen as opposed to high in your chest so that your stomach expands with every in-breath and relaxes with every out-breath. You should be able to know if you are doing this right by noticing the movement through your hands. It doesn't matter whether you breathe through your nose or your mouth, just breathe as you would normally breathe while focusing your attention on the rhythm and sound of your breath as it enters and leaves your body. Do this for three to four minutes until you are breathing in a slow, controlled manner and are comfortable with your breathing.

Now we are going to use your in-breath and out-breath to relax each part of your body, in turn, starting from your head and working down to your feet.

As you breathe in, notice any area on your head, forehead, eyes, etc. that may be tense, and as you breathe out gently relax that area by exhaling and saying to yourself, "Relax."

Now as you breathe in, notice any area around your mouth, your neck, etc. that may be tense, and as you breathe out gently relax that area by exhaling and saying to yourself, "Relax."

This time as you breathe in, notice any area around your shoulders that may be tense, and as you breathe out gently relax that area by exhaling and saying to yourself, "Relax."

Now as you breathe in, notice any area around your abdomen that may be tense, and as you breathe out gently relax that area by exhaling and saying to yourself, "Relax."

This time as you breathe in, notice any area around your buttocks or groin that may be tense, and as you breathe out gently relax that area by exhaling and saying to yourself, "Relax."

Now as you breathe in, notice any area around your thighs and upper leg that may be tense, and as you breathe out gently relax that area by exhaling and saying to yourself, "Relax."

This time as you breathe in notice any area around your lower legs, your ankles that may be tense, and as you breathe out gently relax that area by exhaling and saying to yourself, "Relax."

Now as you breathe in, notice any area around your feet or toes that may be tense, and as you breathe out gently relax that area by exhaling and saying to yourself, "Relax."

And finally as you now take a last long breath in, notice any area in or on your whole body that may be tense, and as you breathe out long and slowly gently relax those areas by exhaling and saying to yourself, "Relax."

By this stage every part of your body has become more relaxed, and you will now notice how much slower and controlled your breathing has become.

Try to practice a progressive muscular relaxation once a day.

If you need help in doing this, an excellent piece of equipment that has been clinically proven to help people relax and even lower blood pressure is something called 'Resperate.' You can view it and product reviews by going to www.resperate.co.uk. You can also dowload an mp3 relaxation audio from www.markdawes.com.

RIGHT AND WRONG THINKING

At the end of the day the quality of our life is down to one basic, fundamental thing, and that is the quality of the decisions we choose to make. There are only two ways we can think, the right way and the wrong way. Right thinking produces the right neuropeptides and wrong thinking produces the wrong neuropeptides.

I recently came across the following words of Mother Teresa in a book I was reading called *Spiritual Capital*[24] which I feel captures the context beautifully. Her words are as follows:

> *People are often unreasonable, illogical and self-centered. Forgive them anyway.*
>
> *If you are kind, people may accuse you of selfish ulterior motives. Be kind anyway.*
>
> *If you are successful, you will win some false friends and some true enemies. Succeed anyway.*
>
> *If you are honest and frank, people may cheat you. Be honest and frank anyway.*
>
> *What you spend years building, someone may destroy overnight. Build anyway.*
>
> *If you find serenity and happiness, people may be jealous. Be happy anyway.*
>
> *The good you do today, people will often forget tomorrow. Do good anyway.*
>
> *Give the world the best you have, and it may never be enough. But give the world the best you have anyway.*
>
> *You see, in the final analysis, it is all between you and God; it was never between you and them anyway.*

---

24. *Spiritual Capital: Wealth We can Live By* by Danah Zohar and Ian Marshall, Berrett-Koehler Publishers (2004), ISBN: 0-7475-7047-7.

CHAPTER 12.
MONEY GROWS ON TREES

Do you remember when you were a child and your parents saying things to you like: *"Money doesn't grow on trees"* or *"What do you think I am, made of money."*

Well, sadly, although possibly well intentioned, they were wrong, money does grow on tress and we are made of money, literally. Now I know that sounds strange to you, but let me explain.

If we consider the neural networks of our brains to be like large dense forests of tall trees, and the branches of those trees reaching outwards and upwards, ever closer to the branches of another tree, then you will begin to understand the logic. If neurons that fire together, wire together (Hebb's Law) that means that the more we think in a certain way, the more neurons we attract to that particular neural network. In other words the 'branches' of our neural trees spread out to attract and invite the branches of other neurons into the network. In essence the 'forest' in that part of our mind becomes denser.

So if we condition ourselves to have a wealthier or richer mindset, then it must follow that we generate a larger neural network dedicated to that purpose. Money does grow on trees in the branches of the neurons that make up and expand the network of the neural forest within our mind.

Having or gaining wealth isn't about where you were born or the education you may or may not have had. It is about **YOU**. It's all about you. If you feel *poor* on the inside then you will not attract wealth. For those lucky ones that do, they are possibly very likely to lose it. Research has shown us time and time again that a large percentage of people who inherit money or who win it on the National Lottery are virtually guaranteed to lose it very quickly. This is because they have a poverty conscious mindset.

THE POVERTY MINDSET

Fear of poverty is a state of mind which I refer to as the

'poverty mindset.' In other words our 'minds' have been 'set' to think poverty. They are constantly focussing on lack which becomes the dominant thought pattern. As any dominant thought pattern will attract to it similar thoughts, just as a magnet attracts metallic objects, a person whose mind is dominated with thoughts of lack will attract more thoughts along those lines. They will focus primarily on what they don't have and will begin to notice more the things that are lacking in their lives. As a result, their focus will be so dominated with what they don't have—or are not likely to have, that they will be unable to think about generating wealth.

It is almost impossible to become wealthy whilst the majority of the thoughts that dominate your mind are focussed on lack or poverty. Poverty is a state of mind and nothing else, yet it is a state of mind that can destroy one's chances of achieving riches. Fear of poverty is parasitic thinking that we talked about in Chapter 9. It can eat away at you from inside, destroying the creative imagination and enthusiasm needed to create and generate wealth. Such thinking makes us doubt ourselves and encourages procrastination, the ability to put off until tomorrow that which we should be doing today.

THE WEALTHY MINDSET

To be rich you have to create a wealth mindset. To do that you have to train your mind to look for the wealth-making opportunities that will come your way. You need to visualise your bank balance as having the precise amount of money that you want in it. You need to be imaging cheques coming through the post and not produce negative emotional states when you see bills.

> "Business opportunities are like buses, there's always another one coming."
>
> Richard Branson

When you do this you start to notice more those opportunities that you didn't notice before—but which were always there. By re-programming the way you think and adopting a better focus, you will literally tune your mind in to notice those opportunities, circumstances and situations that will be drawn into your new awareness. Money making ideas and business opportunities will seem to be constantly coming your way. The real truth of the matter is that they have always been there. It's just that you weren't looking—you were tuned into the wrong frequency or you were 'watching the wrong channel.'

One exercise I have done for years is to visualise my wealth as a vertical gauge, like a barometer or temperature gauge. As I relax I focus my attention on seeing the level rising upwards towards my chosen amount. I also become aware of any good sensations that I get and I focus on those too, amplifying them so that I really feel good about what I'm seeing in my mind's eye. I also repeat affirmations to myself in the present tense, such as:

> "I am wealthy beyond my wildest dreams, money making ideas come easily to me every day, I have an abundance of wealth in my life that I am truly grateful for, I am getting richer and richer every day."

I also take every opportunity I can to create good feelings around things that I would like to own. For example, I constantly look at expensive houses and arrange appointments to view the ones I like. That way I get to experience what I want through all of my senses. Sometimes I will simply imagine myself in the home of my dreams to the extent that I can smell the food cooking in the kitchen and I can feel the soft, ample carpets beneath my feet. I also visualise my family there so that I have everything I want in my minds picture.

I go to expensive garages and test drive expensive cars. I like to feel what it's like by sitting in it, smelling that new car smell and seeing myself sitting in the drivers seat. In fact, that's how I came to own my current new luxury vehicle.

You see, everything is created twice: once in the mind and once in reality. And if you have been reading this book, you will have now come to understand the laws and principles of quantum mechanics and the law of attraction, so you now have all of the knowledge and skills necessary to design your life just the way you want it and to draw into your life those things that you want, simply by focusing your mind and your thoughts in the right direction.

I believe that everything that could possibly exist, already exists inside of us. Think about it! Many of the things we take for granted were once only a thought in someone's mind, and that thought had to come from somewhere. The chair that you sit on, the light that you are possibly reading by, the electricity that powers your home and its appliances. Your mobile phone, computer, internet, e-mail, all were once nothing more than a thought in someone's mind. That is proof of the creative process that we all own inside of us. Nothing can exist in physical terms until it has first existed as a thought in someone's mind.

> "What the mind of man can conceive and believe, it can achieve."
>
> Napoleon Hill

This belief is also echoed by Napoleon Hill, one of the greatest and earliest producers of the modern genre of personal-success literature. Hill examined the power of personal beliefs, and the role they play in personal success.

As part of his phenomenal research, which lasted over twenty-five years, Hill interviewed many of the most famous people of the time, including Edison, Alexander Graham Bell, Henry Ford, John D Rockefeller, F W Woolworth, Theodore Roosevelt, Woodrow Wilson and many other successful people to find out what the secrets were to their unrivaled accomplishments. His findings were eventually published in his best selling book entitled, *Think And Grow Rich*[25], which was first published in 1938.

An excerpt from one of Napoleon Hill's speeches highlights his findings:

> *I think if there was ever a time in this country when men and women need to recognise the power of their own minds—when they need to overcome frustration and fear. That time is now. There is too much fear spread around. Too many people talking about depression, who are trying very hard to see if we can't work ourselves into*

---

25. *Think and Grow Rich!: : The Original Version, Restored and Revised* by Napoleon Hill, Aventine Press (10/2004), ISBN: 1-59330-200-2.

> *a depression, or if we can't work ourselves into another world war.*
>
> *Let's get our minds, each and every one of us, as individuals fixed upon a definite goal so big and so outstanding that we'll have no time to think about these things we don't want. Do you know what are the queer things about mankind consist in the fact that the vast majority of people are born, grow up, struggle, go through life as misery and in failure. Never getting out of life what they want. Not recognising that it would be just as easy—by the turn of a hand so to speak—to switch over and get out of life exactly what they want, not recognising that the mind attracts the thing that the mind dwells upon.*
>
> *You can think about poverty, you can think about failure, you can think about defeat, and that's exactly what you will get.*

As I am writing this chapter the television, radio and newspapers in the UK are all reporting on the current state of the economy. Apparently we are on the brink of an economic recession which means that our economy is experiencing negative growth. The consistent reporting of this through all of the media is creating fear in people's minds. Everyone is talking about it and the fear of what could happen is at the forefront of a lot of people's minds. This means that we are possibly working ourselves into an economic crisis by thinking about it and its negative consequences too often. It is becoming the dominant thinking for a lot of people, who are finding it hard to think about anything else. Now, more than ever, is possibly the right time to heed the great man and his words of wisdom.

If you want financial riches in your life, you need to commit your thinking with passion and with fortitude. You need not to be *hypnotised* by the media stories of gloom and doom that we are constantly being bombarded with. This could easily result in you believing that things are a lot worse than they are, or that there is no hope. You also need to go on a negativity fast.

You need to ignore the inner little critical voice that exists inside us that has been pre-programmed to lower your self-confidence and belief in yourself. You need not to let what others say affect you on a deep emotional level. Do not join the *Fellowship of the Miserables*, but become someone who is in full control over their life.

Keep your mind strong. Shield yourself from the parasitical negativity of others. Focus only on the positive. Look for the opportunities that exist that others fail to see and capitalise on them. Become a beacon of hope for those lost in the fog of despair.

To quote once more from Napoleon Hill's book:

> *An individual can create nothing which he or she does not first conceive in the form of an impulse of thought. Following this statement comes another of still greater importance, namely,* that THOUGHT IMPULSES BEGIN IMMEDIATELY TO TRANSLATE THEMSELVES INTO THEIR PHYSICAL EQUIVALENT, WHETHER THOSE THOUGHTS ARE VOLUNTARY OR INVOLUNTARY.

Whether we are consciously aware of it or whether we are not, our minds are constantly working on the thoughts that they filter. They work on a hierarchy of importance so the thought that generates the greater emotional response or reaction, becomes the most dominant. If we are not careful gatekeepers the only thoughts that we end up paying attention to are those that cause us the greatest negative emotion, and which are recognisable by feelings of fear, worry or anxiety.

Become the master of your own mind. By doing that you will become the master of your true destiny. All things are available to you—and it all starts with how you choose to think!

ENDNOTE

In this book we have traveled across continents in search of new research, explored new sciences into how our minds work, gone back thousands of years in time to look at religion and ancient scripture, delved into the microscopic world that is the universal you, gained knowledge from some of the greatest minds that this world of ours offers and gained inspiration from others who have applied this knowledge to become successful or overcome an illness or a disease.

The sacred secret to get you anything you want out of life is to be happy and compassionate. That is the holy grail of life. We can start being happy by being grateful for all that we already have. We can become compassionate by realizing that we are all infinitely connected. We are all made of the same sub-atomic particles and we all breathe the same air.

Life isn't about what happens, it's about what we make happen, how we perceive what happens to us and how we choose to respond. You were not born to be a victim of life. You were born to be a creator of life and benefit from all of its abundances.

In the Bible, Jesus tells the story of the mustard seed. The story goes that the disciples ask Jesus what the Kingdom of Heaven is like. And Jesus answers by saying that it is like a grain of mustard, the tiniest of all seeds. However, when the mustard seed falls upon well-ploughed and fertile soil—it can grow into a great tree. This parable draws parallels with what we covered in Chapter 3 with regard to how our DNA is influenced by the environment. Our DNA carries the blueprint for who we become, just as every mustard seed carries a blueprint for a mustard tree inside it. The deciding factor in whether a mustard tree grows tall and strong, or whether it grows small and withered, is the environment where the seed is planted. This is the same for us also.

I believe that all of the great sages and prophets throughout time have known about these universal laws and the existence of these infinite fields of potential possibilities that have always, and will always, exist in space and time.

So now you have it, the blueprint for changing your life. All you need to do is provide an environment that will nurture positive thinking so that you can effect the changes that you want to happen in your life—now.

Now some changes take longer than others, and that depends on whether you want to grow a sapling or an oak-tree. However, always remember, that just because you don't see changes immediately, that doesn't mean that changes aren't happening. It is well documented that those who give up are normally very close to success.

The race belongs to those that stay the course, not just those that come first. We all run at different speeds. Some are sprinters, some middle distance runners and some marathon runners. For some change will be immediate, for others it may take a little longer. How deep your groove is and how motivated you are to get out of it are two factors that will decide the speed of change.

A positive focus on life, combined with unwavering belief, faith and knowledge is the magical mix to creating the life you deserve for yourself.

Mark Dawes
November 2008

ABOUT THE AUTHOR
MARK DAWES

Mark Dawes is a successful businessman, a much sought-after consultant and possibly one of the most inspirational and motivational speakers and trainers in the UK today.

As well as being a National Sports Coach, a Cognitive Hypnotherapist and Master Practitioner of NLP (Neuro-Linguistic Programming), he has studied and researched many other fields of personal and professional interest including Positive Psychology, Cognitive Behavioural Therapy, Neuro-Associative Learning, Stress and Combat Psychology and Quantum Mechanics.

Mark has had a varied and interesting career including service in the Royal Navy and as a Hostage Negotiator. He has also worked as an Expert Witnesses with regard to the use of Reasonable Force, with his evidence used in a report by The House of Lords and House of Commons Joint Committee on Human Rights. He has also appeared on Sky and BBC news as well as various radio programmes.

His enthusiasm and commitment are infectious and he is always committed to going that extra mile in the pursuit of excellence and happiness.

If you are interested in attending one of Mark's training courses or seminars on Quantum Thinking visit his web-site at: www.markdawes.com for more details.